Menus, Munitions
and Keeping the Peace

Menus, Munitions and Keeping the Peace

The Home Front Diaries of
Gabrielle West
1914–1917

Edited by

Avalon Weston

PEN & SWORD
HISTORY

First published in Great Britain in 2016 by
PEN AND SWORD HISTORY
an imprint of
Pen and Sword Books Ltd
47 Church Street
Barnsley
South Yorkshire S70 2AS

Copyright © Avalon Weston, 2016

ISBN 978 1 47387 086 4

The right of Avalon Weston to be identified
as the author of this work has been asserted by her in accordance
with the Copyright, Designs and Patents Act 1988.

A CIP record for this book is available from the British Library.

Printed and bound in England
by CPI Group (UK) Ltd, Croydon, CR0 4YY

Typeset in Times New Roman by Chic Graphics.

Pen & Sword Books Ltd incorporates the imprints of Pen & Sword
Archaeology, Atlas, Aviation, Battleground, Discovery,
Family History, History, Maritime, Military, Naval, Politics, Railways,
Select, Social History, Transport, True Crime, Claymore Press,
Frontline Books, Leo Cooper, Praetorian Press, Remember When,
Seaforth Publishing and Wharncliffe.

For a complete list of Pen and Sword titles please contact
Pen and Sword Books Limited
47 Church Street, Barnsley, South Yorkshire, S70 2AS, England
E-mail: enquiries@pen-and-sword.co.uk
Website: www.pen-and-sword.co.uk

Contents

Acknowledgements

I would like to thank the organisations and individuals who have contributed to the publishing of this volume. Without the BBC series *Great War Diaries*, which featured Gabrielle's story, I would never have known her diaries existed. They now reside in the Imperial War Museum, London, who sent me photocopies. These convinced me their story was worth telling, and then Pen and Sword offered to publish them.

A thank you is also due to Anthony Richards, who has written the foreword, which stresses how valued the diaries are by IWM as an example of personal testimony. Perhaps we should all keep diaries? It seems you never know what will be of interest to later generations.

Alexia Clark, of Museum in the Park, Stroud, has been very supportive, and I am grateful to her for permission to use reproductions of Joan Mary West's pictures, the family quilt and other family documents.

The Rotherwas Support Group (who are co-ordinating the factory history), the Society of Brushmakers' Descendants, Sherborne School for Girls, and Stroud Local History Society have all helped me unearth useful facts.

Final pieces of the story came from the Cadby Hall archive, parts of which are held in both Hammersmith Library and the London Metropolitan Archive.

Many thanks, of course, are due to my West cousins, who searched archives and cupboards, and boxes under beds, and came up with, hitherto unknown to me, original materials and photos, including the pre-war diary volume. I think we are all pleased that Great-Aunt Bobby will have her own memorial.

I am grateful to my editor, Linne Matthews. I knew nothing about how to work with a publisher. She chivvied and encouraged and guided, until I was able to deliver the complete manuscript to her.

Thanks are due also, I feel, to the London Freedom Pass scheme. Travelling wherever I needed to throughout the city, to look up and check facts, would have been very expensive without it.

vi

The Story of the Diaries

A cousin and I, on separate sides of the country, watched the BBC Series *Great War Diaries*. One of the diarists was a Gabrielle West. My cousin emailed me.

'That couldn't be Aunt Bobby, could it?'

I followed the idea up and discovered that the diaries were in the Imperial War Museum in London, and were indeed written by our great-aunt. The archivist I spoke to on the telephone told me about two interviews that Gabrielle had given aged eighty-nine, when she offered the diaries to the museum. Finally, I discovered, thanks again to my conversation with the archivist, that as the diaries hadn't been published, as Gabrielle's eldest descendant, I held the copyright.

Shortly afterwards, a parcel of faded photocopies arrived in the post, and I found that the diaries had never even been transcribed from the originals. There is a handwritten note included in one volume: 'Note 1977: Standish House is still a large Hospital, I hear. Perhaps the Head would be amused by this if it is not wanted by your department.'

I set to and produced a typescript. What emerged was the story of how a young woman, badly missing her favourite brother, Michael, who had just gone to work in the Indian Education Service in Bengal, wrote the diaries as long letters to him, giving him her account of her war. She posted them to him at regular intervals.

My cousin and I also went to the museum and listened to Gabrielle's interviews on cassette tapes. To add to the story in the diaries, written 1914–1917, we were able to hear, in her own voice, the reflections of an 89-year-old on her younger self and those wartime adventures.

The last volume of the diaries, for the Armistice, is missing, so other cousins were asked to search. What emerged was not the diary for 1918, but a diary for June and July 1914, up to the outbreak of war. This, so recently rediscovered volume for pre-war 1914, demonstrates vividly what an unexpected event the war was to the general population. Aunt Bobby didn't give it to the museum as she didn't feel it was relevant. A hundred years later, it adds immeasurably to the story, painting a picture of a world about to disappear, and the life of an energetic, under-occupied youngest daughter of the vicarage, teaching Sunday school, visiting relatives and finding her life rather frustrating and boring.

Sadly, a hunt for the last wartime diary volume produced nothing, nor did anything emerge in the examination of her brother, Dr Michael West's, papers at the University of Warwick. The search did, however, produce many old photographs; an account of Gabrielle's elder sister's Victorian upbringing, typed by their mother, Florence; a quilt of scraps of fabric of family importance, also made by the sister but finished by their mother; watercolours; plus a multitude of other facts that have added substance to this book.

I hope, as editor, I have blended these well enough to present a picture of my Great-Aunt Bobby and her war that does her justice, and is both amusing and useful. Very few took her seriously while she was alive. She was a splendid and kind aunt, and this is her contribution to history.

Foreword

Since 1969, the Imperial War Museum has developed an archive of private papers relating to individuals from every kind of background, dating from 1914 to the present day. Largely unpublished, these letters, diaries and memoirs written by servicemen and women, as well as civilians, during wartime, now number well over 20,000. Each collection effectively tells a unique story of a person's wartime experiences, and within this growing store of personal testimony are written records that inevitably stand out as particularly evocative examples. One such highpoint are the diaries of Gabrielle West.

Gabrielle, or 'Bobby', as she was better known for most of her adult life, recorded her wartime experiences in often daily entries, scribbled in notebooks that are now preserved in IWM's archive. As with the best collections of private papers, the writer's personality shines through, and in the case of Bobby's diaries, the reader is easily drawn into her world of the British home front during the First World War. Bobby was determined to contribute to her country's war effort despite the very understandable need to earn a living at the same time, and her initial voluntary work alongside her mother at local hospitals eventually led to paid positions further afield in munitions factory canteens, and ultimately, as one of the first Women Police officers.

Bobby's descriptions of attempting to achieve results in these various jobs, despite being faced with keen but hopeless volunteer workers, badly behaved Munitionettes and the general prejudice shown by both sexes in that era towards women in positions of responsibility, make for an entertaining but extremely instructive read. Bobby's pluck and determination, assisted by her best friend Buckie and loyal dog Rip, shine through every page. Many of the diary entries are extremely amusing at times; her account of being entertained by an aged watch-keeper during an air raid is particularly memorable, while her suspicions towards the working classes frequently raise a smile. However, there remains a dark side to her story as well, with Zeppelin raids bringing death to the very doorsteps of England and the constant danger surrounding munitions work reminding us that the war was an ever-present threat lingering in the background to everyday life.

It is this combination of humour and historical importance that make the diaries so significant. They remain one of IWM's most valued collections of private papers in relation to the First World War, and this publication of the papers in their entirety for the first time is therefore extremely welcome.

Anthony Richards
Head of Documents and Sound,
Imperial War Museum

Introduction

Where did the West family come from?

We don't know everything for certain, but a piecing together of records and family stories produces the following possible history.

This West family were never aristocrats or landowners, or even gentry. The earliest record of them is of an Aaron West, born in 1745, who had a brother Moses, a shoemaker, and two other brothers, Samuel and David, who were thought to be brushmakers from Tadley, near Aldermaston in Hampshire.

BRUSHMAKERS

In love and unity may we support our trade
And keep out those who would our rights invade.
Slogan of Independent Society of Brushmakers

Brushmakers are an interesting craft group. It was an apprenticeship trade. Early brushmakers worked in small groups of four around a pan of hot pitch. They were literate and were said to buy a newspaper between themselves each week. By the 1700s, they had already developed a mutual support system called the Society of Brushmakers, which amounted to, but wasn't allowed to be called, a union. Brushmaking was an insecure craft, but there were brushmaking centres throughout the country.

By 1747, a system called 'tramping' existed whereby an out-of-work brushmaker could take a 'blank' from his local branch and tramp a specific route, a circuit of the brushmaking centres. There would be a contact, at an inn in each town on his list, where he would get his blank signed, get work if it was available, and get paid for the distance he had walked. If there was no work, he would move on to the next town and inn on the list. If he walked the whole way (one route was 1,210 miles), and got back home with no work, the society paid him relief.

(Thanks to Ken Doughty, of the Society of Brushmakers'
Descendants, for this information.)

Aaron migrated to London. Whether he 'tramped' or not, we don't know. No story exists of his parents or earlier origins. As the family became more middle class, they may not have wanted a too detailed memory of their past.

Aaron was said to be a bit of a preacher. By 1777, he was married to Elizabeth Williams and helping her keep a school in Southwark, in London. He died in 1799. In his will he left half his estate to his wife, and a quarter each to his son Ebenezer and daughter Elizabeth. The will mentions his share in his brother David's store of wood in the 'brush cover way'.

The son, Ebenezer, was apprenticed to a measure maker but did well by marrying Jane Johnson, one of the better-off pupils in his parents' school. He is also said to have, accidentally in an auction, bought 42 High Holborn in London, where subsequently he and his wife ran a toy shop, in those days, a sort of gift shop. Ebenezer's sister Elizabeth also ran a school in Bow.

When her mother died, Jane, Ebenezer's wife, who came from rather grander people in Durham, inherited some money. The West family moved on and up.

By 1805, they were Baptist, and are registered as such in Dr Williams's Nonconformist register. Ebenezer's and Elizabeth's births are recorded there, as are those of Ebenezer's two sons, Ebenezer junior and Charles.

By 1821, Ebenezer had abandoned the trade of measure making and is listed as a 'Dissenting Minister', running a small school in his house in Chenies, Buckinghamshire. There is a plaque in the current Baptist chapel there, over the pulpit, commemorating his fifteen years of ministry. The school prospered and moved to bigger premises.

Ebenezer junior took over his father's school when he was only eighteen, and made a success of it. The other son, Charles, Gabrielle West's grandfather, followed a different path.

49 Great Ormond Street, 1882 – Dr Mead's house.
Wellcome Library, London

The Hospital for Sick Children, Great Ormond Street, London, depicted in a wood engraving, 1872.
Wellcome Library, London

Charles West, 1816–73
Founder of Great Ormond Street Hospital
for Sick Children

Charles is always said to have wanted to be a doctor, but the family being Baptists meant he was barred from Oxford and Cambridge. Having been apprenticed to an apothecary aged sixteen, he got his medical education largely abroad. In 1852, he founded the Hospital for Sick Children at 49 Great Ormond Street, London. The house was once that of Dr Mead, who had been the court physician, and had a beautifully decorated interior with high ceilings and painted panels on the walls. An engraving exists of the doctors treating children in a ward set up amidst all the gold paint and elaborate wall panels.

Charles West, photographed by G. Jearrard.
Wellcome Library, London

Dr Charles West published many books, including *How to Nurse Sick Children,* all profits of which went to the hospital. There was another, more informative book, intended for mothers rather than nurses.

The Mother's Manual of Children's Diseases is full of reassurance as well as useful facts. It gives, for example, infant mortality figures for various countries in Europe, and expects mothers to be intelligent enough to understand. However, it has to be said, Dr Charles West didn't approve of women doctors. In his book *The Profession of Medicine*, published in 1896, there is the following passage.

> First as to consultation with women doctors. No one can feel more strongly, or have expressed himself more decidedly than I as to the inexpediency of the practice of medicine by women, a pursuit for which I regard them to quote our late lamented President as 'physically mentally and morally unfit'. However, the public and the Government have thought otherwise. The duty incumbent on the medical man in such circumstances is to treat the female doctor not only with the courtesy due to a colleague but with the special consideration due to a gentlewoman.

xiv

INTRODUCTION

> It is often said of him that he fought with everyone, both professionally and personally, but perhaps men of vision have to fight to achieve their dream. His dream has certainly endured.

In 1865, Dr Charles West also founded a school in Bournemouth, called Ascham House, for delicate children. This was a commercial enterprise. Fees are quoted as 100 guineas a term in about 1900. Both Dr West's children were involved in it. Margaret, his daughter, was an early headmistress, and she wrote later in his obituary: 'He gave me my school training.' She could say little more, as family legend has it that she resigned and became an Anglican nun when her father took a French mistress, whom when he was widowed, he did marry. Margaret is said to have felt the insult to her mother very dearly. Charles West also became a Roman Catholic, which led, he certainly believed, to his being excluded from authority in his own hospital.

So Miss West, the headmistress, became Sister Margaret, the Anglican Nun. She subsequently worked in South Africa in the Community of the Resurrection, Grahamstown, and founded another school there.

The Reverend George West, Dr West's son and Aunt Bobby's father, was a Doctor of Divinity, who gained his degree from Oxford. Before entering the Church, he had an architectural training and continued to design buildings. He was an authority on Gothic architecture and had

Watercolour painting of the barge Margaret, *by Joan Mary, Bobby's sister, on the canal near Stroud. Aunt Margaret was a force to be reckoned with in the lives of the vicarage Wests. The painting is now in the Stroud Museum.*

published on the subject. When his sister Margaret had the disagreement with her father about the French mistress, and his consequent neglect of her mother, she left the school, and George was bullied into taking over.

There were, fairly soon, financial troubles. The school was combined with another in 1903, and the Reverend George became headmaster of both. However, in 1907, although he retained an interest in the school, he retired from it and became the Vicar of Selsley, a village near Stroud in Gloucestershire, until he retired in 1921. He died in 1927.

In 150 years, the West family had radically changed their social class. The descendants of Aaron, the tramping brushmaker and dissenting preacher of the 1760s, became the thoroughly respectable Anglican vicarage family of the 1900s.

Bobby's early years

Bobby was born on 13 September 1890 at the school in Bournemouth, two days before Agatha Christie was born just along the coast in Torquay, a not dissimilar English seaside resort.

Gabrielle West, diarist, pictured in 1891 as a baby sitting on her mother's lap, surrounded by her older siblings: Dr Charles West (far left), dentist; The Reverend George Herbert (to the right of his mother), vicar; Dr Michael West (far right), philologist; and Joan Mary, artist and ceramicist.

INTRODUCTION

Christened Gabrielle Mary West, she was the youngest of five children, which, as she remarks in 1979, was 'very moderate for those days'. Her maternal grandmother, Gabrielle, after whom she was named, had at least ten children.

We have a good idea of what Gabrielle's childhood was like, as her elder sister, Joan Mary, left a vivid description of her own childhood, written in 1948 for a Women's Institute talk, from which this extract is taken:

I am a Victorian, born in 1883, in the reign of the good old queen, whom we then venerated. In fact, I remember getting rather mixed up about the first hymn I learnt. I sang, 'children all should be, good, obedient, meek as she'.

'No,' says Mother, '*he*'.

'Well,' says I, 'Which do you mean? Victoria or Jesus?' …

I had a series of nursery governesses. The pretty ones never stayed long – they

Joan Mary West.

talked to the masters. Then I went to the boys' school for my lessons and we came down and played football and brigands. I once shared a desk with Gladstone's grandson. …

After being educated at the boys' school, my godmother thought I was becoming a tomboy, so I was sent to a select girls' school to learn to be a lady. …

There was only one (privileged) day girl, the doctor's daughter from Christchurch, 3 miles away. She came on a cushion-tyre bicycle. Our headmistress, after seeing her arrival, requested her never again to appear on that vulgar machine. But within a year, we were all mounted on pneumatic tyres, invented by Mr Dunlop, and rode decorously, two by two, in scarlet blouses and blue skirts, into Boscombe to Battle. The crocodile on bikes!

Extract from *A Victorian Childhood*, J.M. West, 1948.

(See Appendix 1 for the full text)

Bobby lived at Ascham School until 1907, when she was seventeen. It was at this school, meant for boys up to fourteen years, that Bobby got almost all the education she ever had. She and her sister were fully integrated into the school. A family quilt exists with a patch labelled 'Bobby's blouse Ascham'.

The family quilt.

In 1907, the family moved to the vicarage in Selsley, where her father became the vicar. The living was in the gift of the Marling family, who were distant connections. Charles, Bobby's eldest brother, had Marling as a middle name. The West family were to some extent the poor relations and continued to have money troubles, but nevertheless, they had the status of being the vicarage family. When commenting on the extent of her father's household in 1979, Bobby says, 'We never aspired to a coachman.'

INTRODUCTION

I visited Selsley while researching the background to the diaries. I had wondered about all the people mentioned in the pre-war diary. How did they interrelate? Once there, the close connection between the families was obvious. The 'Park' where the Marlings lived was adjacent to the new church they had built for the village, and the vicarage backed on to the Marling estate, just beyond. Seeing the geography made it much easier to understand the claustrophobic feel of a few families living in each others' pockets, which is so well conveyed by that first, pre-war diary.

By January 1906, Bobby's elder sister, Joan Mary, has gained various certificates and is teaching Art at Sherborne School for Girls. She is paid, at this time, £30 a year, which is an improvement on the £5 she was paid the previous year as a student teacher.

Her mother Florence writes, 'They speak warmly of her and hint at giving her a better post. It is not so bad to earn £30 but it does not pay her expenses of dress, as the greater part will go on journeys.' The following year, she gets a raise to £50, plus board.

In 1906, Bobby also joins the school as a pupil, and stays only for a year. Sadly, Florence's account of Bobby's growing up has not survived. It is easy to speculate that it was felt that she too, like her sister, needed some time in a girls' school to civilize her, having had, in her case, all her education in her parents' boys' school.

Gabrielle Mary West's name on Sherborne School's admission register for 1907.

In 1979, Bobby is asked about her schooling, and a clear hesitation can be heard. The listener feels she can't bring herself to admit she only attended Sherborne for a year. The interviewer then moves on to what she did after school.

'At eighteen, I came home to the vicarage. When I got back it wasn't long before there were rumblings of war.'

In fact, it was seven years. Those years of work in the Selsley parish seem to have blurred in her mind. The reader can get a clear idea of what she was up to from the diaries of June and July 1914.

Bobby spends most of her young adulthood as a daughter of the vicarage. Her brothers and sister all feature in the diary, but she was by far the youngest, almost ten years younger than her oldest brother, Charles. She was closest to Michael. He was just two years older than she. They were said to be inseparable as children until Michael learned to ride a bike. As we know from her elder sister's account, it was some years before girls got to ride bikes. It is to this favourite brother that the diaries are written, and then posted to him in India.

By the time the First World War starts in August 1914, all Bobby's brothers are launched on their careers. Charles is a dentist in London, George junior a clergyman and actually working in Germany, Michael has set out for India, and Joan Mary, Bobby's sister, is teaching art.

Bobby remained at the vicarage, where she lived the clearly proscribed life of the vicar's daughter, helping her mother, the vicar's wife, by running the Sunday school, visiting the sick and supporting her father in his parish work.

She was never happy sitting still and doing nothing. All her life, she had a little dog of her own. In 1914, it was Rip, who features often in the diaries and always went to work with her. She loved horses, had her own pony, Diana, whom she drove in a governess cart and managed to take with her to both the hospitals she cooked in. When returning from a frustrating two weeks' visiting grandparents, she writes, 'Tomorrow I shall be hard at work cutting the hay, which I want to get stacked before the weather breaks.'

Bobby's mother, and therefore she, were members of the local branch of the Red Cross in Cheltenham, which, as she records in her taped interviews, led to her involvement in the First World War.

'None of it would have happened without the Red Cross. It all began with them.'

INTRODUCTION

Before the reader starts on the diaries, I offer a brief biography of their recipient.

Michael Philip West, 1888–1973

Michael was educated at Marlborough, and Christ Church Oxford. In 1914, he joined the Indian Education Service and became Vice Principal of Dacca Training College, which is in East Bengal, now Bangladesh, and near Calcutta (as it was then).

In 1917, conscription was introduced, and finally, on 30 July 1918, Michael joined the 49th Bengal Regiment as a second lieutenant. He is recorded in the Army list in 1919 as 'released', so his war service was limited, and he probably never left India.

Bobby's brother Michael, sitting atop an elephant in a watercolour painting Bobby sent to him in India.

After the war, he returned to his job as Vice Principal of Dacca Training College. He published much, and is best known for a popular series of TEFL textbooks, *The New Method Readers*. In 1953, he published the General Service List (GSL) of English words, which was updated and reissued in 2013 as the New General Service List (NGSL) of English words.

A nice quote from him comes from a 1988 article by M.L. Tickoo, who met him in London while studying. Michael West said to him, 'Young man, get back to your classroom as soon as possible. It can give you many more answers than I.'

Michael also wrote a detective story under the pen name of Clara Stone, who writes in the 'first person'. It is almost a

Michael in his uniform.

parody of Agatha Christie, but Clara has rather more get up and go than Miss Marple. There are echoes of his sisters in her character.

I include details of the 49th Bengali Regiment, in which Michael West served in the First World War, because it is a little unusual.

Also known as 'The Double Company' or 'Bangali Polton', the 49th Bengali was a short-lived but interesting regiment. It was raised in 1917, when more troops were needed, and disbanded by 1920. It was the only completely ethnic Bengali regiment, and was composed largely of the elite of Bengal (the bhadralok, the gentlemen), who hoped the creation of such a regiment would add force to requests for self-government. They had Indian officers (VCO, viceroy's commissioned officers) but the British officers with the King's Commission remained superior. The regiment was sent to Mesopotamia, not to fight, but for garrison duties. There was much illness in this field of war and the story is told that on one inspection, only sixty-five men were found fit for duty, the officer defining his squads as 'the whooping cough squad', 'the measles squad' and 'the scarlet fever squad'.

Hansard says of it: 'The regiment was not well reported on whilst on field service in Mesopotamia,' but when serving in Kurdistan, it was said they showed 'commendable endurance'.

Kazi Nazrul, the national poet of Bangladesh, served in the 49th. Their war memorial is in Kolkata (formerly Calcutta).

Death in Cranford

Mystery readers are too often starved of literacy with their thrills. They will welcome this first novel of gentle crime and detection which is something new and of considerable distinction. When one of the inhabitants of Pitchley— a village with social conventions as strong as those of Mrs Gaskell's Cranford—is found dead in her bed, murder is suspected. Miss Clara Stone decides to solve the mystery in her own way. Using a technique acquired during her career in an Information Service in London, she discovers a surprising number of skeletons in her friends' cupboards.

Jacket design by
FREDA NICHOLS

13s 6d net

The Clara Stone book, Death in Cranford. *The drawing of 'Clara' is by Bobby's sister, Joan Mary.*

Who is Clara Stone?

A self-portrait

Death in Cranford

CLARA STONE

Miss Clara Stone herself seems surrounded by an air of genteel mystery. We are informed that she was born in 1892 in a village in South-Western England where her father was Vicar; that she served for three years as assistant mistress in a private school for girls, then worked in a Press-Cuttings and Information Service in London; that she returned from this to a village not far from her birthplace, where her hobbies are cookery, gardening—and the study of her human environment. This is her first novel.

HUTCHINSON

The Diaries

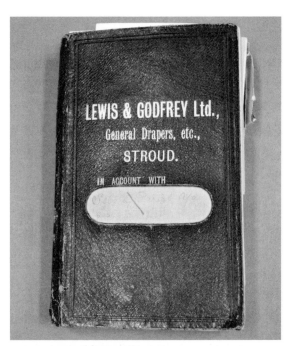

LEWIS & GODFREY Ltd.,

General Drapers, etc.,

STROUD.

IN ACCOUNT WITH

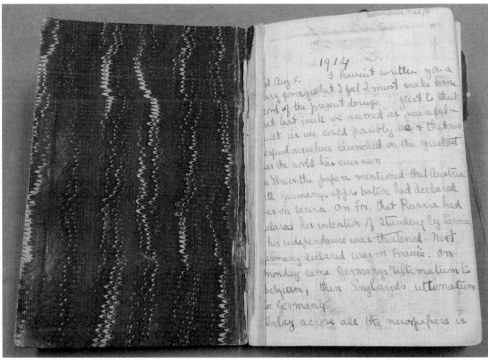

document. 7142/6

1914.

d. Aug 5.   I haven't written you a
ary for ages but I feel I must make some
cord of the present doings.   Just to think
at last week we seemed as peaceful +
uiet as we could possibly be & that now
e find ourselves launched on the greatest
ar the world has ever seen

n Thurs. the papers mentioned that Austria
th Germany, approbation had declared
ar on Servia. On Fri. that Russia had
clared her intention of standing by Servia
her independance was threatened. Next
ermany declared war on France. On
monday came Germanys "ultimatum to
elgium, then Englands ultimatum
o Germany.
Today across all the newspapers is

1914

I am afraid this diary won't be as interesting as the others. I am writing it as much to occupy myself as to interest you. So it is to be hoped it will do a little of both.

Wednesday, 10 June
After seeing you off, I shopped until lunch, which I had with Charles. When he had gone to Dulwich, I went to a cinema at Notting Hill. I have since discovered that the coaching marathon was just going off from Hyde Park, and I might have seen it. That's the second time I've missed it, out of sheer bad luck.

The cinema was perfectly idiotic. I and a woman and a little boy of about five were the only people there, and of course, instead of going where the little brat would not be heard, she must needs come and sit down next to me, when the little beast talked unceasingly from start to finish.

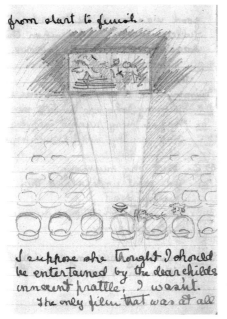

The empty cinema.

3

I suppose she thought I should be entertained by the dear child's innocent prattle. I wasn't. The only film that was at all good was one of the murder of Julius Caesar. Whereupon the dear child struck up as follows:

DC: Mummy who are the tall men?
M: They are very wicked dear.
DC: Why are they wicked Mummy?
M: Hush dear.
DC: But why Mummy?
M: You can't understand this picture dear.
DC: Why is the white man running about?
M: Hush dear.
DC: Mummy, Mummy the silly white man is falling down the steps.
M: Hush dear.
DC: Isn't he a silly man Mummy?
M: Yes dear.
DC: He is a silly man isn't he Mummy?
M: Hush dear.
DC: I don't like this picture.
M: Hush dear.
DC: I think it is a very silly picture.
M: Don't be a baby dear.
    (exit me)
DC: Why is that girl going away?
M: Hush dear.

And I might have been watching the marathon.

Saturday, 13 June
I have omitted my arrival at the Johnstons' and my doings on Thursday and Friday, as they weren't at all interesting, even to myself. [The Johnstons were family friends living in London.]

Mr J. took me and two girls called the Miss Maunsells to Maidenhead, where we took a boat and rowed up the river. It was most glorious weather and we had a delightful day, having lunch and tea in the boat. We went through the famous Boulter's Lock, and quite a long way further. Mr J. ate three jam puffs at lunch, but otherwise nothing very interesting

4

occurred. He wore a very remarkable panama hat, large, white and floppy, which blew off at intervals and had to be hung out to dry. In the boat it looked astounding enough, but in London, walking to the station, it was the wonder and admiration of everyone we passed.

Sunday, 14 June
We had intended to go to the Zoo to see the new Mappin Terraces, but a most fearful thunderstorm came on so we had to give up the idea. It was a great pity. I'd have liked to have seen them.

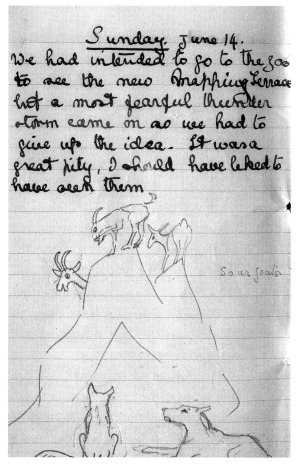

Drawing of animals on the Mappin Terraces, London Zoo, which featured an artificial rocky cliff made of concrete, and were opened in 1913.

However, it cleared up later, and after tea we went to a cinema (just imagine it, on the Sabbath!). I felt a bit guilty, especially as the films were somewhat French, but it was most refreshing after teaching in the Sunday school for goodness knows how many weeks.

Tuesday, 16 June
A friend of the Johnstons came to tea on Thursday. She is one of the head sisters at the London Hospital, and when I told her I knew a nurse there (Evelyn G.), she invited Mrs J. and me to tea. We went today and she showed us over the hospital. Not all of it; that would take a lifetime, but part. She tried to get Evelyn to tea, but she couldn't be spared, so she first took us to her ward so that we could have a talk, but the silly thing was so shy of Mrs J. (that old frump) that she scuttled off as soon as we had said 'How do you do'. Coming back, I caught hold of her again, but she wouldn't stop, so I hardly had three words with her, silly idiot.

Miss Hubbard showed us an operating theatre, lecture hall, children's, men's and women's wards, and also the Hebrew wards, where they have the ten commandments in a tiny metal case on the door post and the Passover unleavened bread on the wall. There was a Jewish rabbi there, too, who looks after the sick peoples' religious needs. Then we saw the mothers and babies, such funny little beasties, some of them only three days old. They are all taken and bathed twice a day in another room; what happens if they get mixed up I can't think, as there were ten or twelve of them, and all very much alike. It was really most interesting, as it is supposed to be the most modern hospital in the world, and the largest.

Coming home, we were just crossing Cockspur Street when my hand was violently shaken by Mr Tetley! He was fearfully smart in a top hat etc., and just going out to dinner, so owing to that and the fact that we were in imminent danger of being run over every minute, we didn't talk for very long. It is extraordinary; I only know two or three people in the whole of London and yet I always seem to be meeting someone I know. Last time it was Percy, and the old music mistress from Sherborne.

The Johnstons have a Dutch boy as 'parlour maid'. He is such a little weirdity. The other day I asked him to talk Dutch to me, so today he began, after many blushes, to recite in Dutch. Between each line he said, 'Oh I cannot. It is so silly.' But he obviously was immensely proud of himself.

Before he came to the Johnstons he was a waiter in a little hotel. He told me, 'The cook was always drunk and oh so dirty, so dirty. When she was not drunk she was a *ver goot* cook, but when she was *dronk* she did sit on a chair and say, "Franz cook the dinner," and I do all the work. Oh it was not nice – no, and there were little brown things, what do you call them? In Dutch it is "*krik*". I will look.' (He then produced a dictionary and looked up '*krik*'.) 'Oh that says black cherry – that not it, that something nice drink is it not? No? Ah, "beetle", "black beetle", that is it. *Krik* – black beetle.'

After this performance he confided to Miss J. that he did dream many nights ago that he would some day talk to real ladies and gentlemen. 'And now it is true. My clothes are not yet good enough to be taken for a chentleman, but someday, someday perhaps.'

When he first arrived in London he went on his evening out to the Tube station at Piccadilly and asked for 'Two seats, ah you are stupid, two seats, two seats for Picalili for the performance! for the circus! for the animals.'

Thursday, 18 June
Miss Johnston and I decided to go and explore Wardour Street, and all the funny foreign shops down in that part. As we went out, Franz was just issuing from the back door for his afternoon out and Miss J. said, 'We are just going down to your favourite haunts in Wardour Street, Franz.'

He put on the most inimitable air, and with his little nose in the air said, 'I, I go not *there*. I go to Harrods to have my hair dressed!' We did feel crushed.

This afternoon we went to a matinee, *The Land of Promise*. Irene Vanbrugh and the great actor Godfrey Tearle were in it. It certainly is very good, all about Canada and life on a farm.

Land of Promise
by Somerset Maugham

The play opened in London at the Duke of York's Theatre in February 1914. It was scheduled to tour in Canada in March that year, but the Canadian authorities were so vociferously indignant at its representation of backwoods Canadian men as violent and uncouth that the tour was cancelled. Almost a million UK citizens had gone to Canada from the UK from 1903 to 1909, among them Bobby's uncle, Charles Whittard, whose wife, Aunt Alice, and children, Stuart and Netta, Bobby will shortly meet in Exmouth.

Our only trouble was two old ladies just beside us who kept up a running fire of what I suppose they thought was a very witty sort of criticism: 'Oh she is going to light the fire. … Well I never, she won't ever make it draw if she does it that way. … She's put enough tea in the pot for twenty, and the water can't have boiled in that time, I'm sure.'

At last, after several withering glances, they subsided, more or less – chiefly less.

Miss and Mrs J. are about the laziest people I've ever met. I don't know which is the worst. It isn't merely that they won't work, I can understand that, but they are too lazy to play either, and never go outside the house if they can help it.

This is their programme for the day.

8.30 Breakfast, for which they are always late. Till about 9.30, Miss J. sits vegetating at the table long after she has finished eating. Then she goes upstairs to complete her toilet. (She always comes to breakfast in a tea gown with her hair down.) After this she watches the servants to see they do their work right. She tells me she finds this very exhausting.

Meanwhile, Mrs goes by Underground to the grocer to order food for the day and returns by Underground. In the afternoon, they stay at home and languish, and ditto during the evening unless, with a mighty effort, they Tube to Selfridges or Harrods, where they spend one and a half or two hours drifting around but never buying anything. Of course, going to the theatre is a different thing, and is only done after much thought and mental agony as a concession to the visitor.

Friday, 19 June
Mr J. (dear Georgie) suggested, as I was leaving for Exmouth this morning at 11 and would not get in till 3.30, I might like some sandwiches. However, Mrs J. had not the least idea of exerting herself to the extent of ordering any, though there were two hours in which to get them done, so she said with the utmost calm, 'I thought Miss West wouldn't need anything. She will get in at 4 and can have a good tea, and as well, I don't think there is anything to make them of.' And though George pressed the matter and I didn't discourage her, she just refused to do anything. I don't think I ever struck anybody much ruder. As if she couldn't have given me a hard-boiled egg and a slice of cake or jam sandwiches, or even have sent round to the shops for a sausage roll; it

wouldn't have taken ten minutes. I really believe laziness like that is a positive disease. By the time I got to Hawksley [Gabrielle's maternal grandparents' house in Exmouth], you can imagine I was distinctly peckish as all I got was a bun at Salisbury.

Saturday, 20 June
Grandpa is certainly a very trying old person with his everlasting 'Can't hear' and 'Can't see'. Also, he seems to take delight in letting one jump up ten times when once would do. Instead of saying 'Give me my pipe and ashtray and matchbox and pin', he asks for the pipe and then waits till you have sat down again and just begun to read, and then asks for the ash tray, and then waits till you are settled once more before he demands the matchbox, and so on.

Grandma is such a pathetic little shadow of what she used to be. Sometimes when Grandpa is out of the way she brightens up and is more like her old self, but while he is about she hardly opens her mouth, she is so afraid of him bellowing at her, 'What is it dear? What are you saying? I can't hear anything you say, you mumble so, wow, wow, wow, wow. What is it?' Then she gets quite pale and trembles before him. I wish he was a little kinder to her, nasty old pig.

Sunday, 21 June
At supper we had a most instructive discourse from Grandpa. 'You know I can't see at all and now I've lost my pin. I am so helpless, I am perpetually losing things. Bertha, can you find my pin? I am obliged to use a pin because the little meat I do eat lodges between my teeth and I am obliged to remove them with a pin.' (Does so.) 'I find it difficult to masticate my food now. I have two or three perfectly sound teeth but they have nothing underneath them, so they press upon the toothless gums beneath. It is a very painful process eating my food now.'

(It is for the spectators.)

'I can't eat this meat at all. I shall be obliged to give it to the birds.'

(The meat is now dropped from his mouth into his glass, where water is poured upon it to soften it for the birds. I shall probably get that glass tomorrow.' (Memo, to learn not to drink during meals.)

Sunday afternoon, went out for a walk. Nothing but couples. Came home again.

The Pin

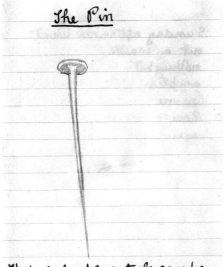

The 3-inch long giant pin.

This valuable article can be utilized for a variety of purpose
1) To clean the ears.
2) Pick the teeth
3) Clean a pipe.
4) Clean the nails.

Five couples, arm in arm.

Sunday afternoon went out a walk.
nothing but couples.
Came home again

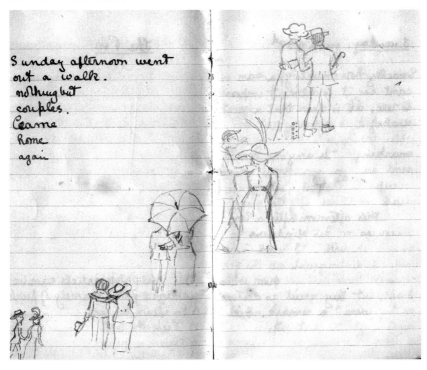

Wednesday, 24 June

My coat and skirt is a great success and was awfully useful in London as one can't wear cotton there. It is grey, checky and trimmed with blue ribbed silk. [A small sample of the fabric is still in the original diary.]

The buttons are rather pretty, like an uncut cameo stone, that is to say, black underneath with a layer of grey on top.

Sunday, 28 June

If I had realized what a deadly rat-hole this is I would never have started keeping a diary. One might just as well keep a diary during a three-week rest cure. Never mind, you must wait till I get home on Friday and then perhaps there will be something to tell.

As there is no Exmouth news I am going to hark back to Selsley and tell you about Diana's lessons in the art of backing. [Diana was Bobby's pony and a fairly recent arrival at the vicarage. She features often in these pages. Having use of a pony and trap gave Bobby independence, as

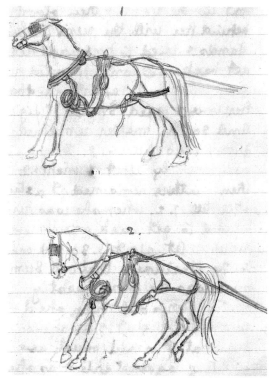

Diana in harness.

getting one's first car would today. As we discover, she takes her everywhere she can, along with Rip, the dog. When working in wartime London, she swaps the pony and trap for her bicycle.]

After the mess she got us into at Preverstone, I made up my mind that it was time she learnt a little on the subject, so I got Old Summers [head groom for the Marlings, at the Park] to come up one evening and give her a lesson.

He harnessed her and brought her out in the yard, and then stood behind her with the reins in his hands and tried to persuade her to get back. Diana planted her four legs firmly apart, laid back her ears and said, 'Shan't'(fig 1, page 11). And so the matter remained from 4.40 till 6.03. Then she gave way by about 6 inches, and there matters remained, at a standstill till 7.02, when she was persuaded to get back a few more inches. At about 7.30, she came to the conclusion that Old Summers is the most pertinacious old man she'd ever struck, and at 7.35 she decided that it wasn't much use fighting against fate, and as she didn't want to stay up all night, she'd better give in and her attitude changed from fig 1 to fig 2. She was then backed triumphantly round and round the yard, and then put in her cart and backed up and down the drive till about 8, when I was at last able to get my supper.

Summers is the most extraordinarily patient old bird I ever met. Fancy standing from 4.40 till eight o'clock behind a nasty little beast of a pony and never losing his temper once, simply saying, 'Get back my beauty there, get back my pretty girl', like an old clockwork doll. No wonder he's got a 'Wonderful way with an 'orse', as Mrs S. [Summers] expresses it.

Wednesday, 1 July
Having been invited to a big garden party by Mrs Ley, I went this afternoon to do my farewell call.

When the maid answered my ring, I asked in the most approved style, 'Is Mrs Ley at home?'

'Yes she is,' said the maid, 'at least, it depends who you are.' I said with great dignity that I was Miss West. 'Oh, then she is not at home,' she announced, and shut the door in my face.

As a matter of fact, I think the explanation was quite simple. They were about to have a party and the maid must have been told not to let in promiscuous callers, only the invited guests, but I think she might have done it a little more elegantly.

Thursday, 2 July

Aunt Alice arrived and is staying with Netta at a boarding house down by the sea. She has just recovered from an operation and seems to be ever so much better, if not cured of her complaint. She is still as fat and voluble and gobbling as ever. I understood about one word in every six, but as she never requires any answers to her remarks, she just sat and gobbled, and I just sat, so we were both satisfied. Netta is a nice little girl; a bit of a prig, but you could hardly expect anything else considering how she has had to take everything into her own hands at a time when most girls are at school.

Aunt Daisy also arrived this evening to look after the grandparents for a week.

It is the funniest thing imaginable to hear Aunt Alice and Aunt Daisy on the subject of each other's children. Aunt Alice says that, of course, Aunt Daisy is full of theories on the upbringing of children and always says everyone's children are spoilt, whereas her own – if she would only believe it – are the most pampered little brats alive.

Aunt Daisy says that Aunt Alice seems to think that no one outside Canada knows anything about anything. According to her, they can't even bring up children properly in the Old Country, whereas – well! If Netta and Stuart are specimens of Canadian children, Aunt Daisy will be in no hurry to cross the Atlantic.

Friday, 3 July

As I arrived from London, I knew nothing about the trains home, so yesterday went down to find out about my journey today. I discovered by far the quickest and most comfortable route is to go across to Starcross in the ferry, and then go straight to Bristol by GWR instead of having to cross Exeter. I therefore arranged to do this, in all innocence, fondly imagining that it was quite the proper thing to do.

But when Grandpa found out, my word, there was a circus. He stamped and raged and gesticulated, and yelled for Bertha and Charlotte until I really thought he would have an apoplectic fit. He said no one had ever gone that way, and I should inevitably be drowned and should never get home at all, that Bertha and Charlotte ought to have seen that I didn't arrange these extraordinary performances, that, of course, Grandma never did anything, or she would have seen to the matter etc. You never saw such a frenzy in your life. Then, when he found my cab came at 2.30, he got up another agitation and ordered dinner at 12.30, until Aunt Daisy intervened. After that he took to coming to the dining room every half hour to know if it wasn't lunch time, and to say that someone had better see to it for, of course, he was so blind he could do nothing.

I assure you, it felt like heaven when I was at last ensconced in the cab en route for the ferry. The horrible journey was made without the least trouble, and I arrived home at about 6 to find that father had come home from Harrogate very sorry for himself as the waters had disagreed with his liver.

Tomorrow I shall be hard at work cutting the hay, which I want to get stacked before the weather breaks.

Monday, 6 July
Percy has made Mother a present of a patent automatic feeder for poultry.

The automatic poultry feeder.

The idea is that they shall only get two or three grains at a time and shall work even for those, and in this way are prevented from getting too fat. There is a little wire cage full of corn, which acts as bait, B. Whenever a hen pecks it, two or three grains fall out of C through some little holes, A. D is a little tin roof to protect the bait from the rain.

So far, our hens haven't quite grasped the principle of the thing, but Percy says that only two of his learnt to work it, and whenever they pecked and a few grains fell, all the other fowls gobbled them up and the poor old peckers never got a look-in. He said they gradually wasted away and perished miserably, but I think that's a little strong.

Monday, 13 July

I don't know what's come over the Park, they [the Marlings] are so amiable. Billy insisted on sending the car for me when I came home from Exmouth, and Stanley is quite amazing. At supper last night he asked most humbly if he might come to see our garden. He offered to give me any flowers I liked out of his in the autumn, and when I said I was short of grass for the goats, he actually invited me to put them on the grass in his new garden; just imagine it. Finally, he told me that Harris could go out with me and the pony whenever I liked. I can't think what's come over them. Father held forth about Dues and Lazarus the Sunday before; perhaps it's done them good.

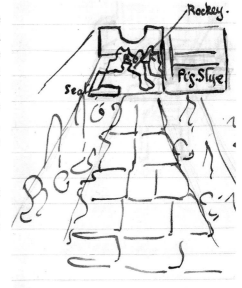

This afternoon he was to have come to tea, but was detained at a political meeting and so didn't come till after tea. He went round the garden and much admired my pigsty bit and suggested a clever scheme for the little square at the end beside the pigsty, which we couldn't decide what to do with.

[The] idea is to have an L-shaped seat and in front of it a little rock garden, and in order to let one see all the view

Plan of seat, pigsty and path.

of Rodborough when sitting on the seat, and to scoop out the wall in a U shape. As he remarked, the ecclesiastical commission will never spot it and it will vastly improve the garden. The seat is to be one of those stiff solid 18C pattern ones, painted white and something like this.

Sketch of the bench.

Thursday, 16 July

Cousin Essie came to tea, also two or three other friends. Of course, she arrived half an hour late and stayed after the others had gone. I'm going round the garden and she has a sudden spasm over the trees in the drive because she says if they were <u>carefully</u> cut, such a <u>wonderful</u> view would be disclosed.

'But you would have to be <u>very</u> careful. I should get one of your brothers to go and pull back a branch and then say, "No, no Charlie, too much. Back a little. Now. That's right, just like that", and then cut off a little piece and go on again bit by bit just like that.' And she waved her fat little arms and danced about and called and waved at an imaginary Charles in the bushes, just like a distracted hen. She is a little weirdity.

Saturday, 18 July

I had my little girls to their annual tea. First they ran races on the tennis court, and then we had tea and quantities of gooseberries. After this, Jessie [the maid who helped with the children] played games and looked after them while I took four at a time for joyrides in the pony cart. They got so excited, and squealed and bobbed about with joy so that everyone turned around to look at them. They paid the railway fares of two little slummers from Bristol who came over to spend the day, and after all the drives were over, I took them down to Stonehouse station in the pony cart and sent them home again to Bristol.

On the way, we came on a huge crowd at the foundry and the fire engine at work, with firemen running up and down the roof of the casting shed, but no smoke or flame I could see. When we came back about an hour and a half later, it was all quiet and we saw the engine starting on its way home, so it can't have been a very big affair, but still, rather an excitement for this part of the world.

Sunday, 19 July

I hear that there were several very spicy titbits in connection with the fire. One of the horses had just come in from a day's work and had a big feed of corn, when he was called out to drag the engine. The result was that the poor beast dropped dead when he reached the foundry. A man belonging to the works got his clothes on fire and jumped into the brook to extinguish them, but even so, was badly burnt. The fire was in the aeroplane shed and close to the petrol tanks, which were expected to blow up at any minute. However, as they refrained and the fire was put out, very little damage was done.

Monday, 20 July

The Philimores [local gentry] have got Bishop George of Lucknow staying with them, and gave a party in his honour. He is a pompous little object. [He is Bobby's first cousin once removed.] He ensconced himself behind a bush and held audiences of one person at a time. When he had finished with any one individual he graciously intimated to them that the audience was at an end, and that he would be obliged if they would inform the next victim that he was ready to receive them, whereupon, No. 1 departed and No. 2 was ushered into the presence. I watched and chuckled from the other side of the bush.

There is a regular plague of garden parties this year – the Philimores', the Jollys', the Bishops', the Marlings', Moreton Balls', Blechleys' and Gilbert Jones's all in the course of the next two weeks. Horrible.

> The Jolly, the Marling and the Bishop families are all distant family connections of the Wests. It seems to have been a much interconnected little social circle. Note the people Michael's elephant is treading on in the drawing on page xxi.
>
> (See the family tree, Appendix 2)

There is horrible wrath at Woodchester. The new vicar is building the most horrible new vicarage in place of that dear old house, and has cut down all the yew trees in the old church yard. Why, I can't think; they weren't anywhere near the house or cattle so they couldn't have done any possible harm. He is a horror.

Mother has gone to Exmouth as Grandpa is ill.

Tuesday, 21 July

Summers gave me a lot of information about the Marlings today. He says it was Stanley and Sir W. who gave him notice, and Lady M. and Jack were afraid to interfere. He was there twenty years and only got 2/- a week all the time he was there, which of course is wretched wages for a head coachman. Also, at Christmas, Lady M. gave him always a woollen waistcoat, no money. Mr Charles was always a gentleman and gave him £1 whenever he came to the Park. He was very upset when he heard Summers was leaving, and said if he had known he would have spoken for him, and that Stanley took very good care that he didn't know till he was going away. Also that Mr Jolly's chauffeur gets 30/- a week, though it is a much smaller establishment. And finally, that he was only given £18 when he left, which was not enough to buy a horse and cab, or do anything useful, and Mr Jolly said if he had treated an old servant so, he should never rest in his bed no more.

Thursday, 23 July

The Park Garden Party. Miss de B. looked so lost that I asked her to tea with Father and me and afterwards repented bitterly. She made piercing and personal remarks the whole time, and no reproofs of mine or Father's seemed to abash her in the least.

'My, what a sketch Miss Apperley does look; why, she gets fatter every day. Who is that red-faced person over there? Is it Miss College? What a feed! My word, I am having a tea but I wish your father would hand me some of that white cake over there. The grapes aren't as good as last year, are they? I've had three ices. How many have you had? Three? My word, just think, six ices, big ones at 6d each; that makes 3/-.'

Friday, 24 July

You said you wanted some of the children's songs etc. so I am sending you some. In *the Old Woman and the Pig* you mount up, repeating the chorus and adding one extra line each time.

[There follows the handwritten words for the following songs:]

The Old Woman and the Pig
The Old Owl Eating Oysters
There Was a Crooked Man
Please Mother, Buy me a Milking Pan
Cock Robin

[See Appendix 3 for the songs' lyrics as written by Gabrielle to her brother.]

This [*Cock Robin*] is a sort of action song in which they all stand round one who lies on the ground as Cock Robin, while one other stands out till verse three, when she comes in as the old woman. The chorus is A E I-O-U, accent on the O, not a,e,i,o,u.

Tuesday, 28 July
All last week I have been so busy getting ready for the sketchers that the diary has had to be quite neglected. Mother was away till Saturday, looking after Grandpa, who had had another rather bad heart attack but is better now. As there are six sketchers coming next Tuesday, I have my hands full. Joan and Mother and Jane are to sleep in the studio, and father

:: :: 1913 :: ::
Sketching Party
— AT —
Sherborne
:: DORSET. ::

aug 7th to Sept 5th

MISS WEST,
Selsley Vicarage, Near Stroud,
GLOS.

Ladies' Sketching Party.

MISS WEST, certified teacher, and pupil of Professor A. W. Rimmington, R.B.A., and of the late Samuel Hodson, R.W.S., proposes to take a Ladies' Sketching Party again, this year to Sherborne, Dorset.

Sherborne is an old world town rich in ancient buildings and quaint traditions centering round its magnificent abbey, ancient school and almshouses, etc., all of which are built of the beautiful orange stone of the district. The surrounding country abounds in lovely little villages, with stately churches and manors nestling amidst orchards and gardens.

A comfortable house has been taken in Sherborne.

Miss West is permitted to refer to pupils who were with her last year, and will be happy to give their names on application.

Terms :—3½ guineas per week (inclusive).
Tuition only 2/6 per hour

A copy of the Sketching Party programme from the previous year.

19

in the study to make room. To complicate matters still further, Mr Husband (who is taking a wedding in Stroud) has asked to be put up one night. So one of the maids will have to sleep out to make room for him. Joan came home this afternoon looking in first-rate health.

> Joan Mary, Bobby's sister, was a qualified art teacher, and had run a successful residential sketching holiday the previous year. As the brochure shows, paying guests came and stayed at the vicarage and were taken around in the pony cart to sketch. During term time, Joan Mary taught at Sherborne School. She wasn't to know when she scheduled her 1914 summer moneymaking venture that events were about to overtake her.

*　　*　　*

Thursday, 30 July
Austria has declared war on Servia and Germany backs her up. Rather a serious state of things. Of course, Father shakes his head and anticipates the end of the world, but there doesn't seem much to be scared of so far.

Friday, 31 July
The newspapers are rather alarming. Russia has declared in favour of Servia, and of course, if she begins to fight, France may be dragged in, then England.

Saturday, 1 August
If Germany does attack Russia, poor George [Gabrielle's brother] will be in rather a hole, as he is taking a chaplaincy at Vilbad, near Strasbourg. I suppose he will be bundled out, being a foreigner. But we haven't had any message from him so far.

Sunday, 2 August
Joan and I went to supper at the Park. We found the Marlings in a fearful state of agitation. Stanley had just arrived post-haste from Bibury, where he had been fishing. He brought news that all the horses in the Oxford district had been commandeered, that Germany had invaded Luxemburg, whose neutrality is guaranteed by England, and that she had also attacked Russia and France.

Percy is expecting to be called away from home at any minute and has wired to Lady M. to come and say goodbye, and altogether they were in a fearful state of nervous flutters.

All the horses in the neighbourhood were listed by the War Office about six months ago in case of need, therefore the Stanley Park horses may be called upon at any minute. Stanley, however, informed Lady M. that he should not let them take Betsy or the Arab, nor of course the pony. But when I said I hoped Diana was safe, Sir Bill said with great asperity, 'You wouldn't refuse to send her, would you?'

The old story of the ewe lamb again. I simply longed to say, 'And the rich man spared to take of his own flocks and his own herds, but he took the poor man's lamb and dressed it for the man that was come unto him' [11 Samuel, 12 verse 4].

Monday, 3 August

Diana wasn't here when the army list was made, so unless someone tells the Remount Officer about her, or he sees her himself, she is fairly safe. I therefore brought her in from the field and put her in the stable, where she will be safe from observation, for Stanley said last night that she would be just the thing for transport work. I hope the beast won't split on me; he is quite equal to it.

Joan has had a telegram from two of her sketchers to say they can't come tomorrow. It will be a tragedy if none of them turn up. No news of George.

Tuesday, 4 August

Two more sketchers have wired that they can't come, and the one remaining one, though she hasn't wired, hasn't turned up. There is one more due on 11 August, but I don't expect she will turn up. It is fearfully hard luck on Joan as she was counting on the money.

Three bank holidays have been proclaimed in order to allow the financial situation to adjust itself. Food is going up, as people are laying in stores already.

Germany has sent threatening messages to Belgium, whom we are bound to protect, so it seems we must be drawn in.

Mr Husband was coming to Stroud to marry [officiate at] an old Bournemouth friend but has wired to say: 'Line blocked by moving troops. Impossible to come.'

Redmond and Carson have both made very fine speeches, promising to sink their differences and that both the Nationalists and the Ulstermen will unite to defend Ireland, so that English troops may be free to go elsewhere.

7.00 pm

The evening paper announces that England has sent an ultimatum to Germany saying that unless Germany will undertake to respect the neutrality of Belgium and Luxemburg, we will declare war.

We have just been round to the Allens, who say the Red Cross camp and display are cancelled. They also read us a letter from their aunt, who has just got back from the South of France.

She was told that the sooner she was away, the better, so took only hand luggage and went to meet a six o'clock train. This did not turn up till 10.30. When she reached Paris, there were no porters and she had to bribe first a little boy, and then a man, to carry her luggage. Then followed a long wait before she could get a train to Dieppe, which she reached about 7.00 pm. On the pier she had to sit on her luggage, first in the broiling sun, and then through a cold night and a rain storm, till three o'clock in the morning, when the first boat arrived. But this was so crowded she was afraid to attempt to get on board for fear of being pushed into the sea, so waited for several hours for the second boat.

Poor George; I suppose he is having similar experiences.

Wednesday, 5 August

I haven't written you a diary for ages, but I feel I must make some record of the present doings. Just to think that last week we seemed as peaceful and quiet as we could possibly be and now we find ourselves launched on the greatest war the world has ever seen.

On Thursday, the papers mentioned that Austria with Germany had declared war on Servia. On Friday, that Russia had declared her intention of standing by Servia if its independence was threatened. Next, Germany declared war on France. On Monday came Germany's ultimatum to Belgium, and then England's ultimatum to Germany.

Today across all the newspapers in huge letters: **England Declares War.**

We went into Stroud this morning. There was great enthusiasm over the Territorials, who are ordered off to the Isle of Wight to train. They were cheered by a tremendous crowd.

What about Mr Asquith's statement that there would be at least six months in which to train them before a war broke out? Why, there wasn't a hint of this war before last Wednesday. Just a week ago!

Everyone is laying in stores. The shops won't sell more than 6lb of sugar, and that at 6d instead of tuppence ha'penny per lb, and 3lb of rice at 4d per lb. The shops are besieged by crowds trying to lay in provisions for the duration of the war. Everyone seems to think there will be a famine in a few weeks' time.

Currency

For those readers not from the UK, and those for whom this coinage wasn't part of their childhood.

Pre-decimal coinage worked as follows:
4 farthings (small copper coins like today's 1p = 1 penny, written 1d
2 ha'pennies (half pennies) = 1 penny (a big copper coin, more like a modern-day £2 coin than anything else)
12 pennies = 1 shilling, written 1/-
20/- = a gold coin known as a sovereign. A half-sovereign also existed, worth 10 shillings.
240d = £1

We also had a hexagonal threepenny bit and silver sixpences, like today's little 5p.

2/6d was known as half a crown, and was a silver coin about the size of a £2 coin.

Many things were billed for in guineas, and still are. A guinea was £1 and 1/-, but a guinea as a coin in its own right no longer existed in 1914.

We virtually abstained from running up prices by buying immense stores. Our hoard consisted of 8lb cheese, 6lb sugar, a tiny ham and tins of cocoa. Some people filled their carriages and motors with sacks of flour, boxes of prunes and raisins, and whole cheeses and sides of bacon. In the morning on our way in we met Mrs Stuart, who told us how wrong it was to hoard food. Later, we met Mr [Stuart] in the Maypole Dairy, buying margarine, and Mrs at the grocers trying to secure a side of bacon!

Last night, Father went to tea with Sir Bill, who told him in an enigmatic voice, 'I suppose you will practise the most rigid economy. We shall have bread and butter pudding and no more macaroons!'

No more macaroons!

We met Eleanor Cartwright, who, when she heard that George was in Germany, said, 'No one is safe abroad,' and plunged into a description of the massacre of twelve German waiters by a mob in Paris. So tactful and encouraging! Charlie Cartwright has volunteered, and Percy Marling, but have had no orders yet.

Thursday, 7 August

We are rather worried about George, who had gone as chaplain to Vilbad. There are such alarming stories about as to the way English people are being treated in Germany – locked up without food, money taken away and how there is a free fight to get into the trains for home.

George arrived safely this evening, none the worse for his journey. On the outbreak of war he was told to leave Vilbad. All his letters were searched, and a long letter about the internal arrangements of motor bikes caused them great heart-searchings. They thought it was about Zeppelins. However, he was allowed to go to Switzerland, where he stayed till the rush of troop trains in France was over. He then came slowly home without adventure. It took four days to come from Switzerland to England, but he doesn't appear to have had any of the hair-raising escapes reported of English refugees in the *Daily Mail*. Anyhow, I'm very glad he is back. Pa and Ma were in a great state about him, and really the reports in the paper were most alarming.

Gabrielle's drawing of men and horses.

We – that is, Joan and I – went into Stroud this afternoon and found that the Midland Railway Yard has been turned into a sort of sale ring. Everyone who wishes to sell a horse takes it there and a party of officers examine it, and if it is suitable, make a bid for it. Those that are accepted are branded on the hoof and sent straight away to the GWR for entrainment. There must have been eighty or 100 horses whose owners have been receiving premiums in time of peace on condition in wartime they shall be sent.

This was the case with the Co-operative Society, all of whose horses were fetched early this morning, and the people whose bread comes from there get none unless they fetch it.

When these are exhausted they will begin to commandeer all the horses they have listed as suitable, amongst them several of the Jollys' and the Marlings'. But as Diana wasn't here in those days, she has escaped being listed, and unless someone tells them of her I don't suppose she will get taken. I do hope not. I should hate to think of her being shot and she is only 14 hands, not really big enough.

Friday, 8 August
We had a great Red Cross practice in consequence of the war. Dr Brown spread out a sterilizer, towels, basins, instruments, dressings etc. on a table and told me and another girl to get ready a side table for the reception of a patient with a sword wound on the head. We had to choose the instruments and sterilize them, get ready the dressings, soap and towels for the doctor, and bandages for the patient. The only thing we forgot was a shaving brush and razor to shave his hair off with. We had great cogitations as to whether rubber gloves ought to be boiled, but eventually we put them in and apparently it was quite right, for he didn't seem to object at all when he saw us fishing them out.

Thursday, 13 August
Joan and I and Miss Streeter (the matron of the hospital where Joan had diphtheria) are off on a driving tour with Diana.

We had a fearful process getting all our belongings stowed into the cart – a bag of corn, a headstall, brush and hay for Diana, biscuits and lead for Rip, groceries and clothes for ourselves; also my umbrella, boot polish, soap, books, sketching things and ever so much more that Joan insisted on putting in at the last moment. However, we all got stowed in at last and off we went to show ourselves to Old Summers, whose pub we passed on the way. [The White Lion Inn, Dundridge Road.] Of course, he found a strap not properly fastened, but on the whole pronounced us 'Very nice, very nice indeed', so we felt distinctly flattered.

> This is the last mention of the Summers family in the diaries. It seems the right place to highlight one of the names on the Selsley war memorial:
>
> > Albert Edward Summers, the son of Mr 'Old Summers', was born at Stanley Park, when his father was a coachman there. The young man joined the 3rd Glosters and was killed in action 25 January 1915, aged 20.

Just outside Cirencester we came on a beautiful piece of roadside grass, so we promptly took Diana out of the cart and turned her loose to feed while we had lunch. Then we went on to the Park, where we drove to the famous spot where the ten drives meet. It is a wonderful place, with the ten wide grass drives cutting through the woods. The trees are magnificent, enormous elms and oaks on all sides. At Cirencester we put Diana up while we went to the church and museum and had tea. I expect you have seen the church, with its wonderful porch. A workman who is restoring it took us up into the room above, which has some very nice sixteenth-century oak. He told us that when the monks had vacated it, it was used as a tavern, until in the sixteenth century it was turned into a court house.

The loaded cart with Diana, three passengers and Rip, the dog.

When we returned to the stables we found that the ostler had more than half-emptied the sack of food I had brought. I'll be bound Diana never ate all that at one sitting. I'm sorry for her little Mary [tummy] if she did.

From Cirencester we drove 7 miles to Arlington, where we found rooms for ourselves and a stable for Diana.

Friday, 14 August

Our next halt was Whitney [*sic*] (where we stayed when you and I and Mother went in the cart to Oxford. Don't you remember *Bleak House* as presented by that travelling theatre?)

As stabling is so dear, we got a farmer to let Diana sleep in a field just outside Whitney [*sic*]. It was inhabited by the most fiendish pigs.

Rip chases off the pigs.

They immediately fell upon the cart and began to bite at the tyres, so that we were obliged with mighty efforts to push it into a shed. After this they processed after Diana, grunting and squealing until she was nearly distracted. Then one of them actually picked up her mane comb and marched off with it in his mouth. Rip was most courageous and when they became too troublesome, charged them in the ribs with all his might and sent them off squealing with terror.

In the morning when I was brushing Diana down before harnessing her, Sister [Miss Streeter, who looked after Joan Mary when she was in the fever hospital with diphtheria] suddenly threw a newspaper over the wall on to her back. You never saw such a skedaddle as she did. When eventually I did persuade her to come back to be finished, she trod on a little white bowl full of water, which went spinning about her feet and sent her flying off to the other end of the field again.

Diana rearing, and pig and bowl.

Saturday, 15 August
We drove on to Oxford and arrived in the rain. We got rooms at a very nice little Temperance hotel opposite the Great Western, and Diana was deposited in the livery stable opposite. Then we went off to see Christ Church and Magdalen Chapel. All the other colleges seemed shut so we were obliged to leave them for another day.

Sunday, 16 August
Went to Christ Church for matins, but were rather disappointed to find

that there was no singing except two hymns, and Strong preached [Dr Thomas Banks Strong, Dean of Christ's Church and Vice Chancellor of Oxford University].

In the afternoon we went on a little drive, and coming home saw a dog fall off the top of a charabanc. Both his front paws were hurt; at first we thought they were broken, but we could see afterwards that it was not as bad as that. We drove him to the vet as he was a biggish dog, too heavy for his master to carry.

In the evening we went to call on Frideswide. She was quite cheerful and prettily dressed, which rather impressed one as I had been led to believe that she was something of a religious maniac. [There is a Pre-Raphaelite stained-glass window depicting Saint Frithuswith, or Frideswide (c. 650–727) at Christ Church Cathedral, Oxford, where her shrine is also located, and this could be what Bobby is referring to here.]

Monday, 17 August
Ever since we have been here, trains full of soldiers, horses and ammunition have been through every half hour, night and day, on their way to the front. This morning we heard that the first trainful of wounded have arrived at Oxford Hospital, and we saw nurses, blankets etc. being hurried thither for them.

After taking leave of the Temperance hotel (which was also a Commercial, and most beautifully clean and comfortable; we found the carpet slipper cupboard), we went to see the Big Game Museum, the Botanic Garden, Wadham, the Sheldonian [Theatre], and the Bodleian [Library]. At the Big Game Museum, Rip suddenly took exception to a lion, and seized him by one ear and gave him a fearful nip.

Rip biting the stuffed lion.

Then we had lunch at Buols [at 21 Cornmarket, Oxford, advertised at the time as 'the finest dining in the West'], of which we did not think very much. In fact, it struck us as distinctly poor; and left Oxford at about two o'clock. We had tea by the roadside at a dear little place called Minster Lovell. There is a very fine fifteenth-century church and the ruins of a castle and priory, besides the most fascinating village street with thatched houses.

From here we went on to Burford, where the innkeeper wanted 3/6d for a bed and 1/6d for breakfast. At last we found cottage rooms and a stable for Diana. But in the morning, the ostler wanted 4/6d for her, although we brought our own corn. I protested loudly and he eventually accepted 2/6d. The idea!

The picture is of the Burford greengrocer's cart. It seems to have had a previous existence as a Victoria [a rather posh carriage, popular in India].

Tuesday, 18 August

Our next stop was Northleach, where there is a very fine church, and the vicar showed us the famous 1623 gilt chalice. There was also a silver one, fifty years older, also the court book, which was begun in the fourteenth century.

While Joan and Sister were looking at the church I drove to the pub for two pints of cider. 'Lor,' said the man, 'be you all alone?' He obviously thought I was about to drink two pints all myself.

Then we travelled on to Chedworth, where we saw the Roman Villa, and drove through part of Cirencester Park, which was full of pheasants and rabbits. Poor Rip went nearly mad.

Diana had had rather more than enough by the time we reached Cirencester and put up for the night.

Wednesday, 19 August

Came home by a little winding road all down the Sapperton Valley – the most beautiful little road I ever saw – and we had lunch on the most delightful village green at Hampton Mansell. The water we got from a spring, which ran through four old stone troughs in succession.

We have had the most sumptuous meals on the tour. Sister has been head cook whilst I was head groom. She introduced us to several new dishes – cheese and onions fried together are perfectly delicious, as is also tinned crab, which I always imagined as a most nauseous mess. Today we had tomatoes, into the centre of which an egg had been broken; you've no idea how pretty they looked, or how nice they were.

Tomatoes with eggs, on a shovel ready to cook.

Our luggage was a good deal larger than on previous trips. Lots of things that would certainly have been voted out if it had been a bicycling tour, were allowed a place when it was only Diana who suffered by it. The result was that there wasn't very much room to sit. In fact, Rip very often couldn't find a corner of any sort and was obliged either to sit on someone else or to stand up on end.

Our belongings consisted of the following:

2 small sacks of food for
    Diana
1 whip
1 umbrella
1 rug
2 cameras
1 cake
1 dandy brush
1 mane comb
2 cloths
1 tin Brasso
1 tin harness polish
1 headstall
1 tin sweets

2 parcels clothes
2 sketching bags
1 basket of groceries
1 bag of oddments
1 dog lead
1 coat
2 mackintoshes
1 bag eggs
1 extra hat
1 loaf
2 bottles cyder
1 Etna [spirit stove for
    cooking]
1 bag dog biscuits.

You can imagine that to stow all that into a small governess cart, which also had to hold three people and a dog, was no small feat of skill. 'Three men in a boat, not to mention the dog' was nothing to it.

Due to the parcels of clothes, each person had a flat one, wrapped up in American cloth, which were put under the cushions of the seats, as being the only vacant space. Sister's was always decked round with pins, and it always seemed to be my unhappy lot to have it under my part of the seat and to receive all the pins. Besides which, she had a coat with the knobbiest buttons you ever saw, which it was also my lot to sit on more than once.

Our picnics were also somewhat adventurous, as on the day when we took refuge from the rain in a little thatched shed and were besieged by three fearsome cart colts who galloped madly round outside and tried to bounce in on us, first from one side, then from the other. Joan was in a panic, I was trying to wave them off with the whip and Sister calmly remained in the shed drinking tea with the coolest unconcern.

By six o'clock we were once more at home. You've no idea how odd it felt to be eating dinner with a knife and fork, and table napkin. I felt rather like Mowgli when he went back to the village after living with the wolves. But it has its compensations; no washing up to be done afterwards.

Thursday, 20 August
Our time will mostly be filled during the day by making bandages and shirts. We have already been invited to three sewing parties and bandage making per week.

Monday, 24 August
Charlie [Gabrielle's eldest brother] went in the afternoon to offer for the Army, but was rejected because of his short sight. George is going to try to get a job as chaplain if he can get Mr Brown and his niece to manage without him.

Tuesday, 25 August
We hear from one of the Stroud nurses that there is a fearful scandal at the Fever Hospital at Cainscross. The matron is too fond of the bottle. There is only one trained nurse to look after as many as thirty beds; all the others are untrained. There is only one bath for all the patients whether

they are in the middle of the disease or just about to be discharged, and they give most dangerous drugs quite recklessly and without asking the doctor first. These abuses have at last been shown up and the matron given notice; so Sister has applied for the job, as it is a much more important position than Stanmore [Hospital]. I do hope she gets it. It would be jolly having her here and I'm sure she'd be a success.

Wednesday, 26 August
Recruiting goes on apace in Stroud. There are as many as twenty or thirty young men outside the office at once. Unfortunately, the sergeant is very busy as he has two places to attend and also has to go to meetings, so he is often away when wanted and, of course, it is very dampening for a young man to toil all the way into Stroud only to find after waiting two or three hours that the sergeant won't be back till the evening, if then. That is what happened to Ernest today.

There have been endless recruiting meetings all over the neighbourhood. Ernest Rigsby (the garden boy) is keen to join if they will take him, so this morning we drove him into Stroud. Outside the Post Office is a notice 'Enquire within for address of local recruiting sergeant', so we went in and not one of the clerks had any idea of his address. One said perhaps we wanted the place behind the Technical School. Thither we went and discovered a small cottage labelled 'Recruiting Sergeant'. There were fifteen or twenty youths waiting for the sergeant, 'who would be back by 10'. We waited till 11 and then fell in with a reservist who told us that was the wrong place, and offered to take Ernest with him and get him through. This he did, and Ernest has to go tomorrow for his medical. Rather a depressing experience for enthusiastic recruits. I wonder what happened to the fifteen outside the cottage.

Thursday, 27 August
Such a shock. Ernest went in today for his medical exam and never came back. He was packed straight off to Bristol Barracks, and all we got was a message from the postman to say he had to go immediately. So we have all had to buckle down to do his work, and mighty hard work too. Cinders to sift, boots, knives, gardening, stable work, potato digging, fetching the butter and half a dozen things as well, but I suppose we must take all this in a day's march in wartime. Am really beginning to feel there is a war on.

Saturday, 29 August

There are mysterious but persistent rumours that Russian troops (two army corps) are being brought across from Archangel to Hull and Edinburgh, and then down to the south of England to be shipped across to France.

Mr Jolly says a friend of his saw them in Hull. Another man saw them go through Gloster [Gloucester]. Another, who works on the railway, said they had orders that facilities for watering 500 horses should be in readiness outside Bristol; another saw twenty-five trains with whitewashed windows pass through Mangotsfield. Another says that when sleeping at Portsmouth last Friday, he heard the sound of men marching for two hours in the night, and in the morning was told that the Russians had gone through. Then Commander Hale says that since the beginning of the war, five cruisers, which sailed under sealed orders, have never been heard of since, and he believes they have been employed in bringing across the Russians. Certainly all trains were stopped for twenty-four hours, which sounds as if something was on hand. It would be a splendid move if true, to suddenly face the Germans with two army corps of new and trained soldiers just where they least expect them, and Kitchener is quite capable of a little dodge of that sort, and the rumours are so varied and persistent it seems there must be some truth in it. People wouldn't invent so many different tales all pointing the same way.

I have just realized that if I don't come to an end at once without more ado, there will be no room for the photos. So goodbye. Let's hope that by the time this diary reaches you, the war will be over and Kaiser William will be spanked and put in the corner.

I have tried, by the by, not to put in much war news except in so far

The conveyance.

Sister making tea.

Lunch on the road to Cirencester.

Threshing near Witney.

35

as it affected us personally in this little corner. All the rest you will get from a special war diary I have compiled for you. I have cuttings from all the different newspapers. It will reach you a week or two after this one, if it doesn't get lost in the post, as so many things seem to nowadays.

The photos are all put at the end because I have only just found time to print them. 'Leaving room' is always unsatisfactory. You always leave too much, or too little.

Thursday, 10 September

As I said, there have been rumours for weeks that large numbers of Russian troops have been brought down from Edinburgh to Portsmouth, and thence to France. Several people have seen porters and stationmasters who have seen them go through, or who have even watered their horses.

Mr Workman of Woodchester says that boats that should have returned from Norway with wood for his sawmills have been commandeered and sent to Archangel [Russia], and for what purpose if not to bring over troops? Mrs Seddon has a sister – a nun in Belgium. There have been Belgian soldiers quartered at the convent. One of the officers told her he had orders to go to the coast and guide the Russians to their ports. In spite of these impressive facts, the newspapers say it is all a hoax.

Friday, 18 September

There has been a wonderful harvest this year. Hay, corn and fruit have been plentiful. We have been inundated with plums and have bottled, made jams and pickled them, even. Apples are 1/6d for 38lbs!

Sunday, 20 September

A Red Cross hospital has been made ready in the Trinity Rooms in Stroud. It holds thirty beds. Most of the patients are Belgians. One English Tommy told Father the following story.

When he was in hospital in France he had opposite him a German, wounded, like him, in the hand. This man got an idea the nurse was neglecting him and when she came one day to dress his wound, he sat up in bed and hit her on the chest with his uninjured hand and swore at her in German. There was an English Medical Officer in the ward at the time who drew his revolver and shot the German dead.

The Belgian family who came to live with the Wests.

Thursday, 24 September

We decided to have two Belgian refugees and put them up in the rooms over the stables – should any Belgians be sent into Gloucestershire. We have whitewashed and scrubbed, and made the rooms look most attractive. Today we heard that fifty refugees were arriving at Stroud at 3. We waited in the station till 5.30. Miss Dickenson, who appeared to be in charge, told us to carry off any who would suit us.

The refugees, when they did arrive, stepped out in a forlorn and apathetic manner, clutching bundles and baskets and numberless babies. All seemed to be in huge families, the smallest lot being six. These we commandeered. Father, stout and had been rather dapper; mother, tall, stout and had been fashionable; two daughters, also stout, red-cheeked; and a yellow-haired, little boy of twelve, not so stout; baby, very stout, pale straw-coloured hair and most bewitching smile.

We got them all into a car, which was waiting to help 'distribute them', and brought them along. While they had supper in the kitchen we flew round and made up extra beds, putting the two girls in Joan's room. It was 8.30 by the time everything was arranged, so as they were dead beat we let them go to bed.

Belgian refugees in Britain

The Germans invaded Belgium on 4 August 1914 because the Belgians had refused them free passage across the country to Paris. As the Germans advanced, a mass exodus of Belgians began. On 14 October 1914, about 16,000 Belgian refugees arrived in Folkestone in a single day. In the course of the war, 250,000 are said to have arrived in Britain. Local committees were set up all over the country. Bobby's description of how the country towns and villages coped is typical of many. What she doesn't record is the Christmas concert given by Lady Marling:

Extract from *Stroud News*, 1 January 1915:

New Year's Eve; Belgians at the Subscription Rooms

By the kindness of Lady Marling, a Christmas entertainment for the Belgians now staying in the district was given in the Subscription Rooms, Stroud, yesterday [Thursday] afternoon. The promoter of the undertaking had the support of a strong ladies' committee, which consisted of the following: Mrs Allen, Mrs J.R. Moreton Ball, Mrs Reginald Green, Mrs Jolly, Mrs F.A. Little, Mrs Matthews and Mrs Paddison, and those are to be congratulated on the great success of the event, which was largely due to the complete arrangements. About 200 of our friends from Belgium were present from all over the district, and everyone thoroughly enjoyed the great treat so thoughtfully provided for them. ...

A little Belgian girl sang the National Anthem, for which she was encored, her country people heartily taking up the refrain. An excellent performance was given by a conjurer engaged by Lady Marling and was greatly enjoyed.

After the war most of the Belgians returned home. Their lasting legacy is said to be represented by a certain gentleman who met a young Agatha Christie in Torquay. He became the model for Hercule Poirot.

Saturday, 26 September

When I went up to read to Sir William [Marling], he said, after hearing of our family, if I would take the books up to him every week he would settle them. Offerings pour in from the village for the Belgians: apples, potatoes, vegetables, a baby's chair and mail cart, toys, clothes, and many invitations to tea.

Their name is Teughels, and their story as follows.

They lived just under the church tower in Malines [Mechelen], when the bombardment began. Fearing it would fall on them, they lived for three days in the cellars and then fled. For two nights they slept in a greenhouse and were so cold that Monsieur went back for extra clothes. Then they went on to Antwerp, and came over to England in a refugee boat. The father was a traveller in wines, wallpapers and corn – a most peculiar mixture.

Friday, 20 November

Belgians getting on pretty well, though they are a bit exacting about their food and raiment [clothing]. Mrs refused a charming little red coat because 'red does not suit fair babies'. The baby is a dear and has already begun to talk English. He says 'Miss West. Puddin. What is dat? Chickuns' etc. Seems very fond of me and waddles after me wherever I go.

Other people's Belgians are not so amiable. Those in Woodchester do their own catering and run up huge bills, buying only the best joints and quantities of butter and eggs. The lady who looks after them says that the only thing that brings a passing smile to their faces is roast pork, so though it is awfully dear, she can't refuse it them.

Most people agree that they are fat, lazy, amiable, and inclined to take all the benefits heaped on them as a matter of course. Our man has got a job as an overseer at a little factory started for the refugees in Painswick. Before he got this he would never do anything for us. When we asked him to help us dig the potatoes, Ernest being away, he always sighed and said, 'Will tomorrow do,' and generally sneaked off or sent his little boy, who is too young to be any use. But they are amiable.

Monday, 30 November

The Teughels have gone, after many emotions. We used to hear many stories of drunken Belgies and always said to ourselves, well, at any rate, ours are very respectable. On Saturday, Mrs went for a weekend with friends. That night, Monsieur did not come home till 1.00 am. When he arrived, he was, as Sarah put it, 'as drunk as a cork'. On Sunday, Monsieur rose betimes and went off on his bike to meet Mrs at Kemble. On Monday, they came back very apologetic. Mrs said to Pa that such a thing might happen even to himself.

On Tuesday, Miss Dickenson sent a rather peremptory note to say the Teughels were to come to Painswick to the house she had found them near his work. I wrote and said they must be allowed to see the house before being removed in this way, but about a week after, the car arrived for them quite without warning. They were in the middle of dinner and didn't want to go, but I think Monsieur was glad to escape from the scene of his transgressions, so eventually they bundled their things together, including the pudding they hadn't had time to eat, and departed with loud lamentations.

Friday, 4 December
Went over to see the Red Cross hospital at Gloster – fifty patients – very smart and working well. Red Cross VADs [Voluntary Aid Detachment] nearly bursting with their own importance. Rather a good story is told of this hospital. One of the VADs arrived by train to do her week's duty at the hospital. She was met on the platform by a porter who told her that there were two patients for her in the waiting room. She found two Tommies, one very ill and very drunk, and the other only drunk. She bravely took one on each arm and marched them off to hospital, where they were put to bed, the second gentleman after much persuasion, he being in an aggressive state of mind. In the morning it transpired they were two convalescents from Bristol who had been let out for the day, had got gloriously drunk and somehow got out of the train at Gloster by mistake. The drink had caused one of them to have a dangerous relapse.

'And I ought to have been back in Bristol last night,' wailed the drunk. 'I shall lose my stripes.'

He was so pitiful that the house surgeons bravely came to the rescue and wrote a note to the Bristol commandant to say that Sergeant Thomas Atkins had been unavoidably detained owing to Private T. Atkins having been taken so ill in the train, and they had been obliged to alight at Gloster and stay the night. I hope the commandant swallowed it. I wonder.

Tommy
by Rudyard Kipling

I went in to a public 'ouse to get a pint o' beer,
The publican 'e comes up and sez, 'We serve no red-coats here.'
The girls be'ind the bar they laughed an' giggled fit to die,
I outs into the street again an' to myself sez I:

O it's Tommy this, an' Tommy that, an' 'Tommy, go away';
But it's 'Thank you, Mister Atkins,' when the band begins to play,
The band begins to play, my boys, the band begins to play,
O it's 'Thank you, Mr Atkins,' when the band begins to play.

I went into a theatre as sober as could be,
They gave a drunk civilian room, but 'adn't none for me;
They sent me to the gallery or round the music 'alls,
But when it comes to fightin', Lord! they'll shove me in the stalls!

For it's Tommy, this an' Tommy that, an' 'Tommy, wait outside';
But it's 'Special train for Atkins' when the trooper's on the tide,
The troopship's on the tide, my boys, the troopship's on the tide,
O it's 'Special train for Atkins' when the trooper's on the tide. ...

Wednesday, 30 December

Joan has brought home a Polish girl who was Music and German mistress at Bentley Priory [Joan was a teacher at Bentley Priory]. Her name is Remizewika. At the outbreak of war, the headmistress meanly gave her notice, fearing she would be mistaken for a German. She has had no news of her people since the beginning of the war. They lived near Przemyśl, where the fighting now is. Being an Austrian Pole she is technically an enemy, though all her sympathies are with the Allies, who the Poles hope will give them their independence. One of her brothers has escaped into Russia and joined the Russian Army; the other was doing his time in the Austrian army when war broke out, so has been obliged to fight for them.

The Jollys and Marlings are convinced that the lady is a spy and won't have her inside their house, so Joan and I had to stay behind on Christmas Day and entertain her.

No one wants them to invite her if they don't want, but they needn't go out of their way to ask after her as 'Your German spy friend'.

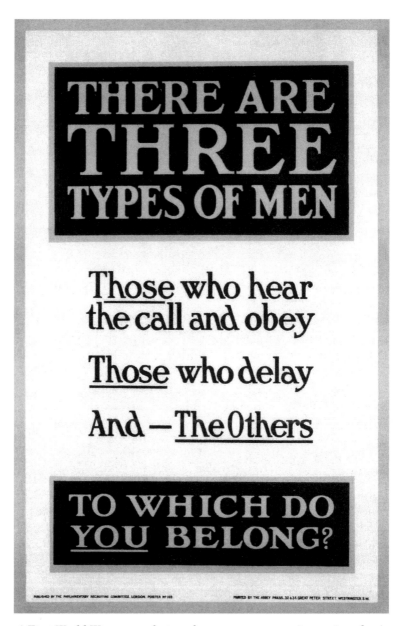

A First World War poster designed to encourage recruitment into the Armed Forces.
Library of Congress

1915

Sunday, 3 January
Miss Remi [Remizewika] has got a job to teach music to some children in Windsor. Last night she read us the descriptions on three of her passports:

> No. 1 Build stout. Eyes brown.
> No. 2 Build medium Eyes grey.
> No. 3 Build proportionate, eyes hazel.

The gentleman who wrote No. 3 was a model of tact, not to say flattery.

Monday, 1 February
Exmouth. Have come down here to stay a month with the grandparents. Deadly dull. The only fun is watching the Hussars manoeuvring on Black Hills. There is a rumour that the submarine that sank the *Formidable* hid in a little bay near here and was supplied with petrol by German spies. Anyhow, there are coastguards and soldiers stationed all along the coast by the hundred. There are hundreds of Belgians here, all fat and smiling, and mostly lazy.

April 1915 [back home in Selsley, Gloucestershire]
Lord Sherbourne has lent his house at Standish for a Red Cross hospital. Five or six Red Cross detachments are to combine to run it. It is a big house on the edge of the woods between Haresfield and Stonehouse. Being so far from the railway, workers are to take it in turns to live in the hospital, a month or more at a time. Mother and I would be included in the Woodchester unit's workers.

Miss King, a very wealthy lady who once lived in it, is to be the commandant. The doctor, who comes from Broadway, is now in residence. He has a wife, a little boy and two girls, who are all living at Standish. He gives lectures, which we all attend once a week. Seems very nice, but a fearful fusser and food crank. Feeds himself on vegetarian

Contemporary postcard of the Red Cross hospital at Standish.

mixtures, has thin toast and coffee without milk for breakfast and brings up his little boy on Captain's biscuits.

Tuesday, 20 April

The matron has been appointed. She is inclined to be meddlesome. She should confine herself to the medical side but instead penetrates into the kitchen and all over the house. She tried to insist on our keeping the dinner plates in a cupboard on the floor. Just imagine lifting piles of plates up off the floor every mealtime. Emma has also been made housekeeper! A very nice person in private life but with no more practical sense than a rabbit, though she has been trained at the Gloster School of Cookery. The hospital is to hold ninety-five patients eighty nurses, house orderlies etc. twelve officials and sisters, and the doctor and his family. So the cooks will have their work cut out.

I am now going twice a week to help clean up. A very arduous job as the house has been empty for years.

The doctor was in a frenzy because of the hundreds of flies. Everyone was given a fly bat and told to go round the windows killing them. The mess after one of these battles was most revolting. Bluebottles don't die at all elegantly when 'bottled'.

So about a fortnight ago I took up the new garden boy and a gallon of carbolic and we cleaned out the stables, which have been used to put up pony carts for the last month and never cleaned. After this, the stream of flies being cut off at the source, the windowsills have been rather less offensive and the doctor a little calmer.

The staff outside the hospital.

Thursday, 13 May

At the last lecture the doctor told us there was no question of the hospital being used for six weeks.

We were just sitting down to lunch today when a wire arrived. 'Standish mobilized this afternoon.' We sent Wilfred up to ask for the loan of the Park car and then to the shops to buy all the bread, cocoa and butter he could get. We got to Standish forty-five minutes after receiving the wire. All the beds were made, and a few nurses collected bread and butter. Cocoa and tea and milk were ready when the convoy arrived at 4.30. Forty men arrived in the first convoy. The Stroud Red Cross Ambulance had only been delivered at Stroud that afternoon. By the time the doctors and sisters and VADs had all had tea it was time to start cooking the supper. Emma Allen had brought nothing but herself. It didn't seem to have entered her head that food was a necessity.

The cooking here is very hard. The doctor and matron have arranged for such a number of different meals. No one seems to feed with anyone else. The doctor and family, the matron and sisters, the VAD nurses, the VAD house staff, the bed cases and the convalescents all feed separately and at separate times. It is most distracting. We have seventeen meals a day to serve! The kitchen staff consists of two cooks, one housekeeper (minus a head) [a sarcastic reference to Emma], two scullery maids and an occasional char lady.

The second cook at present is excellent. She is the daughter of a Painswick boarding house keeper and cooks splendidly, but she is leaving soon and what I shall do then I don't know. You will see her photo later on.

Emma is the most hopeless housekeeper there ever was. Sometimes the stores aren't put out at all, sometimes too much, sometimes too little. You never know what she will do next.* [Added by Bobby many years later in Biro.]

She came in the other day with a basket of beetroots and asked one of the scullery maids to please scrape them! Now beetroots are like the Mammoth:

---

* Emma was not really to blame.
She died a few years later of pernicious anaemia.

46

1915

If the skin be but punctuated before it is boiled,
The confection is wholly and utterly spoiled.
[*More Beasts for Worse Children*, Hilaire Belloc, 1897]

Yesterday there was a commotion because all the milk was pink. Emma had hung the mutton over the milk pan. At my brainy suggestion we scalded the milk and it turned cream coloured again.

Sunday, 23 May
Made a bath can of parsley sauce! And it all got eaten, what's more.

The poor old doctor has put both feet in it. He got hold of two sergeants and three corporals and told them to organize the Tommies and set them regular duties in the wards such as brass polishing, sweeping etc. The sergeants began to do so with great gusto. As one of the Tommies remarked to me, 'These here NCOs aren't in my regiment and they haven't got no business to go ordering me about. No one in the hospital can give me orders except the staff.' So for four days the NCOs organized and the Tommies did absolutely nothing. If they were asked to lift a dustpan, it was, 'I've got a bad arm, Sister, ask some other chap, Sister.' At the end of four days the NCOs gave up in despair and the Tommies promptly set to work.

Eight men arrived and began peeling spuds. Three more appeared to scrub the kitchen, and another to do the grate. Since then there has been a small army every day peeling potatoes, washing cabbage, cleaning knives, polishing taps etc.

Friday, 4 June
Went out as chaperone for a motor drive with four soldiers. Arrived home just behind a new convoy, all Stonehouse cheering us wildly. At the hospital door, four St John's men, and began tenderly lifting my four very convalescent young men out of the car, to the intense joy of all the old hands.

Miss Russell, the good cook, has gone and I have got a terror in her place! This is the sort of process we go through daily:

'Have you made the doctor's pudding, Miss Barnes?'

'Oh Lor', no! What shall I make it of? Shall I put it in the oven? Lor', there isn't room. Can I move something?'

Later …

47

'Oh Lor', I've forgotten that pudding; it's as black as your hat. Ha ha ha. What shall I do now?'

Her jellies won't jell. Her moulds [a sort of blancmange] are all lumps, her cocoa is too strong one day, too weak the next and not enough of it the third.

Monday, 7 June

There are a good number of Scotsmen and Canadians among the wounded. There are six Kilties: Old Jock, New Jock, Little Jock, Big Jock, Canadian Jock and Jock with the Tam o'Shanter. Little Jock of the Black Watch is very fat and dumpy. He and big Jock, who is over 6ft, generally come and help lift down the potato steamer. If you offer him a cloth to put round the handle he always answers, 'No thank you, it'll do with me kilt.' He got into the habit of doing things with his kilt because at the front he had a billycan with no handle and had to get it off the fire with his kilt. Now if ever anyone is taken with a feeble fit and doesn't know how to do anything, everyone shrieks 'Do it with your kilt.'

The other day there was great agitation again because one of the men shot some tiny rabbits, which he persuaded me to cook. He then gave some to a Canadian pal and persuaded him they were rats, and that stewed rat is a favourite dish in Scotland. Great disgust on the part of the Canadian at the filthy habit of the Scotch.

Corporal Lennard of the East Surreys is very depressed. All the men of his regiment have been killed or wounded, except seven. He was behind a sandbag parapet when a bullet hit it and shot the sand into his eye. When I told him Ernest was in the Machine Gun Corps, he said he would give him weeks to live, not more. I hope it's not as bad as that.

We have two gentleman rankers. One wears silk pyjamas; you can tell at once which he is because he is the only one who doesn't say 'Wipers' [Ypres]. He is a Jewish stockbroker and has the most astounding lady friends in motorcars to visit him. I asked him how he had been hit. He said, with a groan, 'I wasn't hit, I've had jaundice and measles and an operation, and I jolly well wish I had been.'

The other gentleman is the 'one with the gold teeth', a foreman from British Columbia, quite a good sort; brings offerings of grapes to the cooks whenever his friends send them him. He takes great delight in nagging the sober Emma. One day she offended him by not saying 'Good Morning', so every time she appeared she was greeted by gold teeth and all the other potato peelers – 'Good morning, Miss Allen, Good morning Miss Allen' etc., until they had made her say it a dozen times. Another day he made a vow that everyone who came out of the yard door should have a gooseberry thrown at their heads. Even the sisters got potted so that the whole yard was bouncing with green gooseberries. Yesterday, Gold Teeth told me how to make flapjacks.

'You just get some flour, you see, Sister, and you mix it up with some water and you put in a bit of soda, you see, Sister, and a bit of salt, and you cook them on a sort of griddle, you see, Sister.' Rather vague!

Then there is Dan Leno. His real name is Wines, but he is so exactly like Dan Leno that nobody calls him anything else. He can be very funny, too. He told me, or rather a friend of his told me, that when he was in the base hospital he was playing cards, and a sister and doctor came round and tied a label on his bed.

'What's that for, doctor?' says Wines.

'Oh,' says the doctor, 'that's to say you're going to be sent home.'

Dan hurled the pack straight at the doctor's head.

'Why didn't you say so before, you blighter?'

Pony (Diana) and cart, with (left to right) Private Buckle, Gabrielle, Miss Russell and Driver Dixon.

There is another good tale about him. We had been inundated with presents of rhubarb. One day, one of the VADs who thought Wines rather frivolous told him very solemnly that he would be glad to hear that the Bishop was coming to hold a service on the lawn on Sunday. Wines looked at her very solemnly for a moment and said, 'Lor', will *he* bring a bunch of rhubarb?'

For the last two or three weeks I have had Diana [the pony] here so that I could go out on drives in the afternoon and sometimes home to tea. Driver Dixon and Private Buckle have adopted her. They clean her harness and cart, and polish her up till she shines like the sun. Sometimes I take them out in the afternoon. Buckle is a farm boy from Northallerton. He thought he would be refused at Northallerton, so he and a friend walked to York to enlist there, but Buckle was refused so tramped all the way back to Northallerton, where he was accepted. He was only two weeks in France when he got shot in the arm. He told me the RAMC men get a very bad time.

'You see 'em go out and pick up a chap and then the stretcher and all goes up in the air and the Germans pick 'em all off in turn.'

None of them want to go back. There is one man doing the new sun cure. He has a large wound on the thigh. They have tried skin grafting without effect so now he lies out in the garden for the sun to shine direct on the wound. It is healing up fast. He says at all events, it is fine weather for lying about and doing nothing.

And then there is Driver Dixon. He is just splendid. He enlisted some years before the war to be a private groom to his master's horses, the master being Captain W. of Cricklade. He went out early in the war and served through that ghastly retreat from Mons, and was wounded during the final battle, getting six bullets in the leg and one in the arm. He was holding his master's horse at the time and by a coincidence, he also got six in the leg. Well Dixon was sent back to Devonport, cured and sent straight back to the front.

He was made a driver in the RFC after this. He served round Ypres and Armentières. One day when changing the position of their gun, a shell killed his pair of horses. The gun went on and he was left to await the new horses and bring them on. He remained behind to take the harness off the dead pair, and while doing this the gas came up. I think he was pretty bad. He is fairly well now, though he coughs badly every now and then.

He told me they covered 20–30 miles a day during the retreat for three days and had practically no rest. The horses didn't have their harness off. Then, after standing ready all night, they fought the battle, which turned the tide. When the horses did get their harness off, the skin came too.

'Oh,' says Emma Allen, 'how terrible, but you know I believe we suffered even more than you did when we read in *The Times* that the whole British Army had been cut to pieces.' Dixon just looked at her. Some people don't seem to have any sense.

As to the Germans, he says the Saxons are quite decent, and when the two lines of trenches are close, Buckle told me the Saxons will blaze away, taking care not to hit. If they once get into the British trench, their first act is to surrender. They used to call remarks to them in quite a friendly way and when they were about to be withdrawn they held up a notice saying, 'Look out, the Prussians tomorrow'. The Prussian Guard and the Death's Head Hussars are brutes, especially to the prisoners.

Dixon said, 'I'd rather shoot myself than be taken by one of them.'

Mother asked him if he had seen any atrocities.

'I haven't seen them doing anything,' he said. 'But I've seen the things they've done. I've seen three wounded men strangled with the cord that holds their identification badge.'

That's why most chaps don't wear it round their necks. They put them on their braces, or round their arms or wrists. He also saw a man taken off by ambulance men to the nearest village. This was during the retreat. When they got there the Germans were entering it and all the wounded were being moved. So they put their man in an ambulance and started back. One got separated from the others and met two Huns, and 'When I saw him again coming back to our unit he was crying with rage. They'd cut off his right hand at the wrist.'

He also told us that the fuss about the lack of ammunition was justified, and that a lot of the ammunition from America was bad and that the fuses flew off as the shell went through the air. That meant that the shell would 'fall fluid', and also there was a chance the fuse might hit someone and go right through him. This was caused by the fuses being brass when they might be aluminium.

Tuesday, 8 June

A fearful fuss last evening. One of the men, Campbell, came home rolling drunk. He had a basket of eggs, goodness knows where he got them, and began handing them round. The sister took them away and began to put him to bed. The doctor, who is very strong on teetotalism, burst in and began a lecture, telling the man he was a disgrace to the British Army and a lot more, no doubt equally true but very ill-timed. The result was the drunk got mad and gave the poor good doctor a shaking up, whereupon the doctor, very scared, rushed off and telephoned for the police. The drunk got hold of a rabbit gun that the Tommies sometimes use and sat on the bed breathing out threatenings and slaughter against all and sundry. The doctor forbad anyone to go into the ward in case the drunk might shoot at them, and he might succeed in hitting one of them. As if they had never seen a gun before!

So all the other occupants sat about disconsolately until about 11.00 pm – unable to go to bed. Meanwhile, the police arrived and explained that soldiers in hospital were not their job, and went away. Eventually, the sister marched in, took the gun and put my lord to bed. This morning, the escort came to take him back to Bristol. Dixon tells me he was a really bad lot and had been kicked out of several regiments for bad conduct, but always re-enlists.

Thursday, 10 June
Aunt Maggie has sent me the most colossal sock, a perfect monster. Enclosed was a note saying she meant to make a pair but all the wool got used up on one, but perhaps there was some poor fellow who had lost one leg and would find it useful. Would I let her know what I did with it. Goodness knows, that fatal last sentence prevents me putting it in the dustbin, the only place it is fit for. Even if there was a man with one leg he wouldn't need a flour sack for the remaining one!

Really, living in a VAD hospital is too agitating for anything! This afternoon the doctor asked me to tea. Fanny Philimore and Miss Benet were there. In the middle of tea Dr W. begins a violent tirade about the cooking.

'The men must have less meat and more green food, also the gooseberries were not properly cooked. It didn't matter about other things, but gooseberries, of all things, were simply poison unless they were well done.' etc.

He got so pink, and danced and stormed like a perfect lunatic. When he had done, I said, 'Well, Dr W., as you know, all the vegetables here are presents. People send a few carrots, two or three cabbages, a basket of leeks, six or seven cauliflowers, and how am I to cook a motley collection like that when we haven't got room on the stove for more than two or three pots?'

'Build another range, then.'

'And where should we put the chimney? As to the gooseberries, I am sorry. I was not able to see to them myself, as you know, my second cook (Miss B.) is not as good as she might be, and although I admit they were not well done, I don't think they were as raw as you think.'

After this, I took my departure.

This evening, when Emma came in, I told her of the stormy tea party and added that I thought it was disgusting to invite a person to tea and in front of two other people to rage at her like that. Poor old Emma was furious, and as luck would have it, in walked the doctor and then the fat was in the fire.

Emma gave it him hot and they fairly had a battle royal. Of course, I wouldn't for the world have had a row, but as Emma was in a way fighting on my behalf, and as I really did think he had behaved very badly, I couldn't desert her. So I said nothing, until he appealed to me, when I said, 'Well, Dr W., I honestly think it was hard lines to attack me in front of two other people in that way.'

Eventually, the supper bell rang so I went to supper, and later, Dr W. sent a message to say he was sorry and hadn't meant any harm, and he hoped it wouldn't interfere with our friendship in the future, which was nice of him.

Life here isn't all beer and skittles. As I said, a few days ago the doctor made a huge fuss because he said the men weren't getting enough greens. All the vegetables are presents so it's very difficult to get enough of anything to go round, and there isn't normally room on the range to cook a dozen different vegetables at once. However, I was determined they should have enough green today so we boiled a whole copperful of cabbage. No sooner was it underway than in bounces the good doctor to know if something can be done to stop the smell of cabbage all over the house. Such is life!!

Miss Russell came back today, joy! I hope I may never see that dreadful Barnes woman again!

For some time past I have been sleeping in a tent. I have borrowed it from Mr Jolly. Miss R. and I sleep in there, instead of in those dreadful stuffy bedrooms. Some brainy person got the idea of pitching tents in the

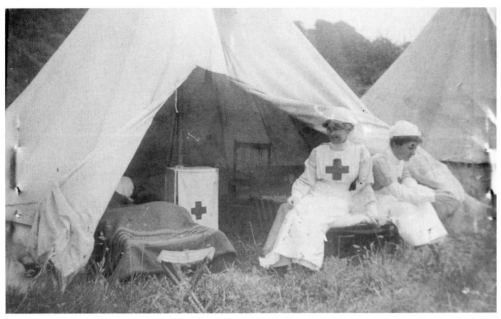

Gabrielle and Miss Russell in the tent.

field behind. There are six of them in all, and they look right out over the
Severn Valley. It is just glorious. That nice Buckle and Dixon put ours up
for us. I shared it for a long time with Miss Russell; now I sleep in it alone.

Sunday, 13 June
The Bishop held a very nice service today on the lawn. All the men came,
except about three.

Monday, 14 June
The men gave a sing-song. It was very amusing. The melancholy corporal
sang comic songs, and one man played most wonderfully on a mouth
organ. I never knew before what a mouth organ could do. Another man
recited a poem of his own, on the murder of a private by natives in India.
He got a £25 prize for it, and it really was very good indeed.

Tuesday, 15 June
Today we took Dixon and Buckle out in the pony cart. He and Buckle
have been so good over the pony. They groom her every day, wash the
cart, clean the harness and get her ready for us whenever we want to go
out, so we thought we must show our gratitude as much as we could. We
drove around by the river, then on the way home we stopped and ate cake

by the roadside as we didn't want to be in for tea, and then we went on again. They certainly seemed to enjoy it no end, and certainly I did. They had such a lot to say and were very interesting.

Buckle confided to me that after tea, they sneak one of the saucepans from the kitchens and go up to the wards, make a fire and have a feed. I asked him what they fed on. He replied, 'New potatoes and rabbits, and all sorts of things'. 'But,' he added very virtuously, 'we always put the saucepan back clean.' So now we know where they go!

Wednesday, 16 June
Drove home to see Mother today and found she had had the most amazing letter from Maud Philimore warning us that Miss King and Mrs Aubrey intend to give us and Emma the sack. Apparently they are dissatisfied with Emma and are afraid to get rid of her alone, so are trying to get round the difficulty by making a complete change. I am very distressed. I was very happy there, and I honestly thought that our services were of value and that we were 'doing our bit'. However, they seem to think otherwise, though I must say it is a dirty trick, making us into scapegoats to screen themselves. While we have been there I can honestly say that the meals have never failed. They have always been in time and always well cooked, with a few minor exceptions, which occur in any household. I should have thought it was a bit of an achievement; all the VADs and the men have said how wonderfully we worked it and how nice the food has been. However, there is nothing to be done except wait and see.

Saturday, 19 June
Today my time was up, so I left Standish and Mother took my place. I wonder if I shall ever go back?

Tuesday, 22 June
I have been back to Standish several times as I had to drive the afternoon cooks over, i.e. Mrs Hallet and Miss Cox. Mother seemed to be getting on very well, and the food, I heard, on all sides, was first rate. But today I found Emma in a state of wild excitement. The blow has fallen.

Miss King informed her and Mother that, 'they no longer need a housekeeper, and of course Mother had been so good, but she couldn't be permanent, and we think your daughter rather young, so we think we had better make a complete change.'

Mother asked why I was too young and they said my cooking had been excellent, 'but then, of course, we think she may find it difficult to keep her scullery probationers in order and prevent flirting with the soldiers.' All of which was just an excuse. The only scullery pro who flirted was Miss K.'s own niece. I waited a long time thinking she would give her a hint about it, but as she didn't, I spoke to her myself, so I don't think I did badly for a young one. However, the fact remains we are ignominiously booted, and there's an end of it.

Wednesday, 23 June
Drove Mother and Buckle and Dixon to Gloster. We put the pony up and then went and had an ice, then went just inside the cathedral, which I was surprised to find Dixon very much appreciated, then to tea at the Oriental, then a cinema and then drove home. I think they enjoyed it; they seemed to anyhow.

Dixon told us of several interesting things today. First, that the life of a gun is about 1,000 rounds, and that the talk about there being plenty of guns at the front and no one to fire them originated from people who know nothing about it and who thought that the hundreds of worn-out guns at the base were waiting for teams. At the Battle of Mons, Dixon's gun fired 700 rounds, with only brief pauses to cool it.

One of the officers in his battery got a DSO [Distinguished Service Order]. A fire broke out amongst the ammunition and he got it all moved and the men cleared out, but as he was getting out of the way himself, a shell exploded and hit him in the back so that he will never be able to walk again. 'And he was a good officer too; he deserved a DSO, if anyone did,' said Dixon with enthusiasm.

He told us the German officers treat their men like pigs; no English private would stand for it.

'What are the English officers like?' asked Mother.

'Oh, they're first rate, only some of these new Kitchener's Army are too young. They're alright, only they haven't had enough experience. It takes years to make a good officer.'

A lot of the atrocities, he said, were due to the drink the Germans got, and their officers encouraged instead of suppressing them.

'In the British Army a man just daren't get drunk. Why, in the retreat from Mons, you mightn't pick an apple off a tree without paying for it even though the Germans were right behind taking everything they could grab. But it pays. All the country people will let an English soldier have anything. Why, the kids come all around you when you stop and beg for souvenirs. They even take your rations, biscuits and things for souvenirs. They aren't afraid of asking for things, I can tell you.

'The Gurkhas, my word, it is a treat to see them. They don't care over much for shellfire, but when it comes to storming a trench they just go out as quiet as anything but all-over smiles, and they come back laughing: and they don't bring no German helmets for souvenirs.'

'What do you mean?' said Mother.

'Ears, bits of fingers, anything like that is in their line,' said Dixon calmly.

Friday, 25 June
Miss K. seems scared. She told Mother she hoped she would come over three times a week to help look after things, and she hoped in August we would come and help them through. Mother replied very coolly that she would probably have to go and stay at Exmouth and didn't think she could be spared in August. Miss K. was in a great state of consternation.

Emma has been given a post as housekeeper at Naunton Park Hospital, Cheltenham, 160 beds. Her sister Clementina, being private secretary to Captain Colchester Wemys, County Director of the Red Cross, has got her the job.

She was very angry at the way we had been treated, and last week had Mrs Aubrey and Miss K. over to Gloster and rowed them about it. Said she would make them have us back, only it would be so awkward for us. So Emma's getting this job is a distinct snub for them. She left yesterday.

The *Cheltenham Chronicle and Gloucestershire Graphic* of 10 July 1915 featured a selection of photographs of the Red Cross Hospital at Naunton Park, describing the set-up there:

> Within the last two or three weeks the big block of council schools at Naunton Park, Cheltenham, has been converted into a magnificent Red Cross Military Hospital, and now accommodates over a hundred cases. It has capacity for many more. Miss Geddes is commandant, and there is a large staff of local ladies. The recreation ground behind is used exclusively for the soldiers at certain hours of the day.

The big Central Ward, formerly the School Hall.

Dinner in the big ward.

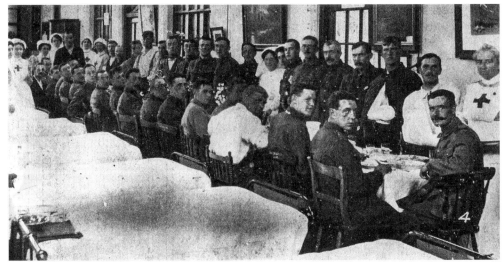

The mess room for convalescents.

The cricket team. They played three or four matches, beating New Court Hospital twice.

Saturday, 26 June

Yesterday Mother went to see Captain C.W., who told her he would give her and me good jobs if we wanted them. The result was that I have had an offer to go to Naunton Park as head cook. I don't much want to be under Emma again but I have accepted, as the officials here have behaved so badly to her and Mother and myself, and some others of the staff.

This afternoon, Mother told Miss K., and added that my being away, she would have to look after the parish etc. and couldn't go to Standish anymore. Miss K. was filled with consternation and dismay. Mother said she nearly wept. Serve her right; she's begun to realize that she has been a bit rash.

Tuesday, 29 June
Buckle and Private Houghton of the Dragoon Guards came over and made my hay. [They grew enough in the vicarage garden to feed Diana and their goats.] We had lunch and tea on the lawn. They confided to Sarah that they had so enjoyed themselves, that they so liked me and Mother, but most of the others were silly old fussers and they were sick of being hustled about by silly women.

Houghton has been at the front since October and wasn't touched. He was finally knocked out by a kick on the knee when breaking in Australian Walers [horses] at Rouen.

Wednesday, 30 June
As Houghton had a bad knee and was the nearest approach I could find to a man with one leg, I gave him Aunt M.'s sock, to his huge delight. He vows he will use it as a sleeping bag. He has written a most delightful note of thanks for me to forward to Aunt M. She will be quite delighted and flatter herself no end, never dreaming how much fun that poor old sack has caused.

> To an unknown friend
> Just a few lines to let you know that I received the sock from Miss West, which I am very pleased with and thanking you for same.
> I remain
> yours
> Private A. Houghton.

We were to have taken Corporal Lennard, the melancholy East Sussex man, and Bombardier Wells to Gloster, but as there was a terrible storm brewing, we drove home instead. Luckily it didn't rain till we got in. Then it began to pour, so we could only sit and talk and have a good tea, bacon and eggs, cake, honey, toast etc.

The corporal had quite a lot to say. He told us he often had to do listening duty in no-man's-land and reckoned to lose three or four men every night. One thing struck me rather.

When a village was occupied by Germans, the Belgian women fled to one occupied by British. The officer in command had to find them shelter, so put them in the kitchens of the house while the Tommies slept in the upper rooms. 'And they were quite happy; they knew they were as safe as a church – an English soldier would no more have dared touch one than fly.'

Doesn't that speak volumes for our discipline?

Bombardier Wells is very big and very fascinating, and very shy. For a long time he passed himself off as the famous Bombardier Wells. No one having heard of an army bombardier before, we swallowed quite innocently for a long time. He told me the commissariat often broke down in the first weeks of the war, and several times he was obliged to eat the horses' oats when the men's supplies ran out.

William Thomas Wells, aka Bombadier Billy Wells, was a famous English heavyweight boxer, British Empire Champion 1911–19. From 1915, he served with the Welch Regiment and for a while after the war, organized physical training for soldiers in France.
Bain News Service/Library of Congress

Both men were both very disgusted at the idea of being put into the blue invalid suits at Standish, which are supposed to be arriving next week. I proposed that if they were, they should change suits every night and then complain they didn't fit. It would create such a fuss.

They told Sarah that one man had a girl friend, a relative, up to see him and she talked to him over the railings. Miss K. sailed down and told her she should be ashamed of herself etc., to his great indignation.

Also, a sergeant from Quedgley, who has been wounded three times, came up to see over the hospital and was sent off. Bombardier Wells remarked, 'I gave Mrs Aubrey a bit of my mind over that. I really couldn't help it.'

This local newspaper cutting is pasted into the diary. As we know, Bobby was a pupil herself at Sherborne girls' school in 1908, and her elder sister Joan Mary an art teacher there 1903–10.

Fraulein von Bissing

Fraulein von Bissing, a relative of Baron von Bissing, who was until recently a teacher at a school in Sherborne, has left the town.

Public indignation at the employment of Fraulein von Bissing and other German women was expressed so strongly that Mr Seager, chairman of the local authority, convened a special meeting to consider what steps should be taken. He stated that 300 men and women of Sherborne had sworn to raid the school unless the German women were expelled.

Communications passed between the authorities and the governors of the school, but the attitude of the townspeople became so threatening that the urban district council refused to accept responsibility if the women remained.

Fraulein von Bissing then left the town and the school is entirely free of German teachers.

Thursday, 1 July

Arrived Cheltenham and went up to the hospital, but of course I didn't do anything as I only arrived about seven. Not a very large kitchen, about as big as Standish. Seven gas stoves and a number of rings, also a hot cupboard for plates.

Naunton Park is a very large modern National School, built on a very spacious scale, with lots of air and sun and all on one floor. The kitchen (once the Domestic Training Room for girls) is some way away from the main block of wards, across an asphalt yard. Jolly in wet weather! Apart from this it seems to make a first-rate hospital. There are 155 patients, and beds for 160. Many of the cases are bad, and a couple dangerous.

Emma and I are in nice rooms about ten minutes away but have all our meals at the hospital, in her office, not with the other nurses.

Sunday, 4 July

This is a truly awful place! My first day was something terrific. In the morning down came a sheaf of thirteen diet sheets, one for each ward and one for the convalescents. I tried my best to puzzle them out.

This is the sort of thing I found:

Ward 1: No. of beds 6   Full diet 4   Low diet 3   Milk diet 1   Total 8??
Two appear to sleep on the floor.

Or I found:

Ward 6: No. of beds 5   Full diet 3   Low 2   Extras 6 eggs.

Now do I count six eggs as well as the regular diet or instead of one diet? Are they all going to be eaten at once or one at a time?

Well, I set them out on paper as best as I could.

Emma has put the low diets entirely in my hands so I and another girl cooked the various items. There were about thirty or forty of them.

Rice pudding, tapioca, sago, Benger's Food [an invalid food supplement], custard, beef tea, soup, poached egg, chicken, fish, stewed fruit, mince and so on and so on.

Then it came to dishing it all up, which took a long time. Then we had to carry it all up on trays right across that awful yard.

While we were running up and down with load after load, the nurses descended on what was already there, like vultures. Ward 8 took Ward 9's poached egg. Ward 1 took Ward 4's chicken, and there was a circus. I was helpless. I never saw such chaos, and of course I was brand new and didn't even know the numbers of the wards. I couldn't do much to save the situation.

Sister Jackson, who is practically matron, descended on me in a fearful fury.

'Why was there no chicken for Ward 4?'

Because Ward 1 sneaked it.

'Why had Ward 1 got eight diets for six men?'

Why indeed?

'Why had I sent six eggs to Ward 6? Did I think one man could eat six eggs at once?'

I didn't know how many men were eating them. Apparently, one man has two for breakfast, two for dinner and two for supper, but how could I possibly know unless they said so?

Well, I was very brave, and when her breath gave out, I said, 'Well, I will try and get them better, but will you please ask the sisters what time they want their orders, and she would tell the VADs that they are to take nothing off this table unless I give it to them.'

Next day was much the same, possibly a shade better. Today things were really improved.

I have started various little schemes:

1. I label each dish Ward 1, Ward 2 etc.
2. I take it all up in one go on the trolley.
3. I have a list and give out one ward at a time and then cross them off.
4. I have a 'sluggard's delight' to keep things hot.
5. I always carry the diet sheets in my pocket so that if there are any complaints I can refer to them. In nineteen cases out of twenty, it is the nurses' mistake.

Thus, yesterday, an angry VAD wanted to know why, when her man was recovering from beriberi, I go and give him rice pudding. I said I couldn't be expected to know he'd got beriberi.

'I said not rice.'

Then I produce the diet sheet – 1 milk pudding. Exit VAD with humble apologies. That sort of thing happens three or four times a day but I think I am always ready with hard facts to prove them wrong; that they'll soon drop it. Anyhow, I see a faint glimmer of hope for me today. They are beginning to be a little cautious.

On Friday and Saturday I thought I never should be able to pull it off, but now I feel at any rate I'll give it a try. I mean to slog away for a fortnight and see if at the end of it there is an improvement. If not, I shall confess myself beaten, but I don't mean to be that if I can possibly help it.

Tuesday, 6 July

Yesterday was much better and today, marvellous to relate, not a single hitch or complaint. Bland and smiling nurses come quietly and take away the dishes, and not a single attempt at a scrimmage. Sister Jackson, who gave me such a dressing down my first day, is all smiles. I like her; she's got such a charming face, and after all, though it wasn't my fault, it really

The hospital ward huts at Standish Red Cross Hospital.

Gabrielle in Red Cross uniform with her food trolley, self-captioned 'Myself GMW'.

was enough to make an angel swear, that first day. A lot of serious cases and you can't get them proper food. I believe it has been much the same since the hospital opened, about a month.

Tuesday, 6 July
Another day of calm, that is to say, there were no ructions, so I really think that I have weathered the worst of the storm. From now on, it seems as if it would be fairly plain sailing, but plenty of work.

I find every day I have to provide:

fish	beef tea
chicken	chicken broth
soup	stewed fruit
nine or ten milk puddings	poached eggs
five or six custards	mince
junket	bread and milk

And half a dozen other little trifles such as buttered toast, stout, cream, lemon etc. Also, anything I can think of to tempt the appetites of the two or three who are so very ill.

My day is therefore something like this:

7.30	Arrive at hospital, sterilize milk, weigh out milk puddings etc.
8.00	Breakfast.
8.30	Start cooking.
9.00	Take round 12 or 14 jugs of labelled and measured milk and Benger's, lemonade, beef tea to each ward.
9.30	Return and with the help of my assistant, cook the dinners.
12.00	Dish up and serve dinner.
1.00	Eat my own.
1.30	Make porridge, Benger's etc. for following day.
2.00	Take round more milk.

After this I am off duty till 5.30.

5.30	Cook suppers (milk pudding, Benger's, soup, beef tea, eggs, etc.)

7.30	Prepare lemonade, butter, meat, milk, eggs, for use by the night sisters.
8.30	Supper.
9–9.30	Draw up diet sheets for following day. Empty the stockpot and refill it, and then I am finished.

Besides this there are perpetual calls for more milk, Benger's, eggs, beef, etc. at all hours, and these have to be prepared and hustled up to the wards straight away.

So you see, I really earn my keep.

I soon saw that it was hopeless for one to attempt to do the full diet as well, so I told Miss A., I would stick to the low and be responsible for them, but she must find another girl for the full. This she is going to do.

Besides this, I run 'the rag and bone yard'. There I keep all the bones and rabbit skins, which are called for once a week by the most horrible old man, and he and I haggle over the price and quality of these treasures. Anyway, I got 5/6d out of him last week.

The work here is very hard and it is dull in lodgings all alone with Emma. I miss our jolly drives in the afternoon and the company of all the other nurses that there was at Standish.

But this is a bigger job and I should be a slacker to chuck it just

Gabrielle's drawing of her bargaining with the old man over the bones and skins.

because of my own personal feelings. I've got to do my bit whether I enjoy it or not; after all, what are my little discomforts compared to what our men have been through? But it is dull here.

Emma isn't getting very well to grips with the problems here. She muddles along, then something goes wrong and she rouses herself into a great state of hustle, hauls things through somehow and relapses again, but she doesn't really go to the root of her troubles and put things right one bit. i.e.: Every now and then, no one turns up to help in the kitchen. Emma rushes around and digs up a scullery pro, or someone to help, but she never takes the trouble to find out how the mistake arose, and in all probability, the same thing happens again the very next day. However, she has several first-rate cooks and so things go on fairly well.

My great trouble is that Sundays are just as bad as weekdays for me. Chicken broth, beef tea etc. has to go on just as usual, and there doesn't seem to be any 'day off' for poor me. I don't see how I can go on working eleven hours a day for ever without any break.

Thursday, 8 July
Emma is in despair. Thursday last, the men in the mess room had shepherd's pie for supper made from some dubious remnants Emma had poked away in the meat safe and then rediscovered several days later. The result was that a lot of the men were very ill all night. The consequence was that I had a dreadful time making albumen water, rice water, arrowroot and goodness knows what, all day.

Emma is on the verge of hysterics and tried to make me throw away some apples I stewed last night, because, forsooth she was 'sure they were sour and would make the men ill again.'

The same thing happened once before, when Miss C. was housekeeper, and some said it was the work of a German spy. There is a girl here about whom they received an anonymous letter of warning, and she was present both times this happened. Another strange thing about it is that the sisters, who ate one of the same pies, were not ill.

I have arranged to have a holiday on Thursday and someone else is going to do my work. I wrote to Buckle, asking him if he would like to come for a drive, and received a charming letter from Houghton saying that Buckle is going on Monday and asked him to write instead, and that he would be delighted to come out. I was very pleased to hear from him but a little surprised that the faithless B. hadn't written.

Ernest goes home for forty-eight hours' leave on Saturday before leaving for the front. I am so sorry to miss him, but it is too late now to alter my plans, but I should have liked to see him again, maybe for the last time, for a corporal of a machine gun does not have the safest of jobs.

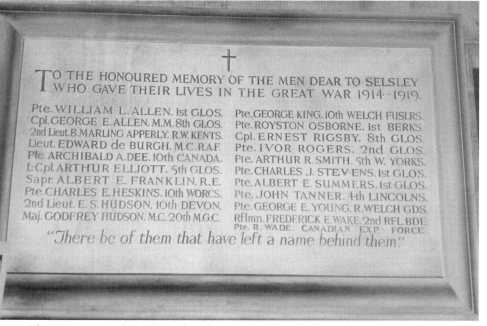

The war memorial in Selsey church.

Ernest Rigsby, the garden boy who joined up on 3 August 1914, was a corporal and acting sergeant in the 8th Glosters when he was killed on the Somme on 25 October 1916.

His younger brother, Enslin, joined the Navy aged fourteen in 1915, and in 1934 was awarded a Long Service Medal.

Another name on the memorial is Private Albert E. Summers, 1st Glosters. He was the son of 'Old Summers', who taught Diana the pony to reverse, and of whom Bobby was so fond. The young man was killed on 25 January 1915, aged twenty.

It is so clear from the diaries that the general population had no idea of the slaughter that was coming.

In the census of 1911, Selsley had a population of 1,877, made up of 464 families. There are twenty-one names on the war memorial.

Thursday, 15 July

I arrived home last night by the 6.40. Found Joan and Pa at home. We got to Standish at 1.30 with the pony cart. Pa and I drove and Joan rode the auto wheel. We took Houghton and Bombardier Wells and drove up to Uley. Of course, we had to walk the hill but I don't think they minded that a bit. The view and the flowers were lovely. We stopped at the farm, put up the pony and then discovered we had no bread, so I went down to the shop for it. When we came back the two soldiers and Father had wandered off, so Joan and I left the food and went to find them. When we came back, behold, a huge pig had just taken a large hunch out of the top of the loaf. However, he left enough for us, but if we'd been a minute later there wouldn't have been much. We gave them a very good tea – new bread, butter, honey, mutton pies, cake from Kung, cherries, raspberries, strawberries and cream – and I think they really enjoyed it.

Rip was very naughty, stole the sugar and pestered us for bits and caused a good deal of fun, so that altogether it was great fun.

Then we drove back to Selsley, dropped Pa and picked up Sarah, and took W. and H. back to Standish. The first thing they said on getting out was, 'When will you be coming back? I suppose we will be gone by the time you do.'

'Oh,' I said, 'I hear you won't be well for three weeks and I shall be back before that. Will you come again?'

'Rather. If you'll take us.'

So I think the picnic really can be written down as a success. It is such a joy to find something one <u>can</u> do to repay them in some degree for all they've done for us. I don't think I ever enjoyed myself more. They told Sarah, while I was talking to Maud and Miss K., 'Do ask Miss West to have us out again, we did have a lovely time.'

They are both such splendid men. I'm really proud to be friends with them.

I came back by the 7.15 and got my diet sheets ready for tomorrow before I went to bed.

Monday, 19 July

A dreadful shock today. At breakfast Emma received a letter from the commandant saying some such as this:

I have given you plenty of time to improve things, but you have
not done so. The kitchen is dirty, the larders are a disgrace, the
men's meals are in a muddle. I must therefore ask you to leave
tomorrow.

Emma showed me the letter and seemed most dreadfully upset, and
announced that she should go at once. I tried to persuade her to stay till
next day, but she would not. Just marched out there and then, and honestly
I can't say I was sorry. She was a sore trial, not only incapable at her work,
but a most boring person to live with.

Of course, when the discovery was made that Emma had gone, there
was a great sensation, and Miss W., the assistant commandant, came to
take her place. Presently, down she came to interview me. As I arrived at
the same time as Emma and lodged with her, they seemed to think I
should go too. I was told that the only part of the kitchen that worked
successfully had been the low diets – my job: and was begged to stay.
Having no desire to throw my lot in with Emma, I graciously consented
to stay.

The assistant commandant isn't bad, but a most dreadful fusser. She
knows very little of cooking, but won't even let you make a milk pudding
without worrying round asking what grain you have used, whether you
are sure the milk is sweet, have you put in the sugar etc.

We now have a chef-in-command, Mr Millington. He has been a great
man and cooked for dukes and even for the late King George, and now
keeps a large and very swanky boarding house. He is running this for a
fortnight. He is a funny little man. He also does catering for beanfeasts
etc. He is to be both cook and housekeeper for a fortnight, at the end of
which time Miss Buckpitt, a head of a school of Domestic Economy, is
taking on the job. She, like Mr Millington, has been working here a day
or two every week and I should think from what I have seen of her that
she is quite nice, and certainly very capable.

Tuesday, July 27
Mr M.'s fortnight has not been pure joy. Wonderful cooking – duck and
green peas for the sisters, with meringue creams, goodness knows what;
and goodness knows what the bills will be either. He began by treating
us all with the utmost deference and always called us 'Madam'. Then it
became 'Young lady', later on, 'You girls', and now, as often as not, it is

'Silly boobies'. His reign comes to an end tomorrow and I shan't be altogether sorry.

Saturday, 28 August
Miss Smith goes for a month's holiday. She is a girl of about nineteen. Very nice and capable, and since Emma's departure has shared my rooms. She does most of the full diet cooking but only works from 6.30 am to 2.00 pm, so the suppers have to be done by someone else.

Sister [the companion of the camping trip] is coming to help in the kitchen for three weeks, and Mother for a week. Miss Buckpitt goes on holiday on the 30th before taking over the housekeeping as a permanency, so we shall need all the helpers we can get. Miss Geddes has got a friend coming to take her place. I hope she will be capable.

Monday, 30 August
Miss Buckpitt has introduced many reforms. We have all cleaned the kitchens and larders, unearthing quantities of dirt and getting ourselves very black in the process. This is a photo [opposite] of us in our spring cleaning get-up. She has evolved some sort of order out of what was sheer chaos. She keeps her workers very much up to the mark and expects a good deal, but she is very good-tempered and quite fair. In spite of the fact she has the work of ten people on her shoulders and that half her workers are as silly and unreliable as they can be, I have never seen her snap or fly out at anyone or vent her irritation on the innocent, as most people in her position would have done.

Friday, 3 September
Miss Bentley, who has taken charge during Miss B.'s absence, is enough to make one weep. She wanders around like a stray kitten and is quite delighted if you give her a nice simple little job like stirring the porridge. But as to ordering up the meals, she is too hopeless for words. She puts up the menu after the meals have been eaten. Every evening, Miss S. asks her what is for breakfast the following day, and she says, 'Ooooh, I don't know!' You suggest bacon. 'Ooooh, yes.' You go to the larder and there is no bacon as she has forgotten to order it, so then we are reduced to fishing out 200 of the precious eggs Miss B. has pickled with such loving care.

Poor Sister has all the work on her shoulders. She has spent her

'On the left is Miss Smith, the girl who does the full diet cooking, a very good sort. Next comes Miss B., then myself, and lastly, Alice, who is the only paid worker in the kitchen. She peels potatoes and cooks vegetables, scrubs the floor etc.'

month's holiday here cooking, and [has] done extremely well. She has to order all the meals and try to make Miss Bentley get in the stores. It is marvellous what a lot she does get through and how well she does it. All the kitchen people are hugely impressed and like her tremendously. But the great people in the office, instead of showing any gratitude, rather imply that they think her a rotter because things don't go so well as when Miss B. and Miss S. were here. Personally, I think they ought to be devoutly thankful that anything goes at all. The meals have always been good and up to time, though the sisters haven't been fed quite so sumptuously, and the night nurses have not always had two vegetables every night.

The hospital sisters were filled with wrath when they saw her in a sister's cap, and sent a message to say that cooks were not supposed to wear such things. They were duly squashed when they found she is a full-blown sister.

Friday, 10 September

We have all been to an entertainment given to wounded, VADs etc., in the Opera House. The place was packed. Part of the programme consisted of amateur acting and songs, which was very good. We have a real live professional as a patient. He has a beautiful tenor and sang *Trumpeter, what are you sounding now?*, *Annie Laurie* and *Keep the Home Fires Burning*. It was fine to hear all the Tommies roaring the choruses. The rest of the time was occupied by The Cingalee company, who were at the theatre that week.

All the wounded in Cheltenham were invited; also nurses, cooks, washers-up, and even the Girl Guides and Scouts, who sometimes help.

One of the cooks overheard one of the VADs in the audience remark, 'Everyone seems to have been invited. Even the cooks and the others are here.' Who are those 'others' more degraded even than cooks?

Sister went home today and I feel very forlorn without her.

Tuesday, 14 September

Mother, Charlie [Gabrielle's eldest brother] and Bessie Davies, Charlie's fiancée, came over for the afternoon. She is very attractive, quite a dear, not pretty but has lovely blue eyes and is very jolly and unaffected.

Mother here helping with the kitchen for a week, so we are having great fun.

Wednesday, 15 September

Everything has been going wrong since Miss Buckpitt went away and at last, in desperation, they sent for her last week to come back. I thought it would be more to the point if Miss C. had come to the rescue and helped Miss Bentley through instead of sitting, hands folded, and seeing everything go to pot, and then recall poor Miss B., who sorely needed a holiday.

Miss B. is by no means pleased at having to come back a week early. She says she begged Miss G. to get a really competent locum, paid, if necessary, and she thinks it too bad of her to have put in the silly old goat, who has undone all that she accomplished in three weeks' hard work. I quite agree.

74

Allow me to point out Miss B. in the centre, Sister on her left, myself at the back, also Mother. The lady with the Red Cross is the third cook, a very good sort but caused some scandal by her flirtations with the patients.'

'Below is a group of patients. In the chair, my pride and joy, and also my cross, Sergeant Goldberg, recovering from beriberi, largely owing to my ministrations. He has to be well fed, but no cereals and no sugar – some problem! On the bench, the professional singer.'

'Sister, the assistant housekeeper who took Miss B.'s place, my assistant, Miss Organ. Above these, New Zealanders who came over to help in the war, and myself, doing a sneeze. With regard to the New Zealanders, one of them told me that during the voyage they were told to pack their valuables in small handbags in case they had to take to the boats – she hadn't any valuables and she didn't think a nightie or a toothbrush any use, so at last she put in a bottle of acid drops and a pack of cards.'

Sunday, 3 October

For the last two days, Miss C. has been doing Miss B.'s work as she had to stay at home and receive her girls, who are just starting their term.

Miss B.'s training school is rather unique. She trains ladies for domestic service, and after training finds them posts. All wear a quaint little uniform: blue cotton dresses, white aprons and a little medal stamped *laborare est orare* [to work is to pray], and caps stamped with the willow pattern. The outdoor uniform is a funny little brown bonnet and a brown coat with three capes. After three months' training and sundry exams the pupils are given a certificate and found a post. The mistress, before her 'lady help' is sent her, has to sign an agreement undertaking to give her two hours off daily and a separate bedroom, afternoon and evening once a week and part of Sunday. These lady servants go by the name of 'Dame of the Household' and call each other Dame Mary, Dame Margaret etc.

Yesterday there was no milk, and Miss Buckpitt had forgotten to tell Miss C. to order the rabbits and fish for me. Today, much the same happened. It was very hot, and I got somewhat exasperated and went to Miss Craster and groused a bit, said I could not cook without materials etc., meaning it as much as a dig at her as at Miss B. She said she would tell Miss B. that things must really be properly ordered, and I really thought no more about it. But today, when Miss Buckpitt came into the kitchen, she stalked up to me like a ramrod and said, 'Will you please let me know, Miss West, what you need for today and I will see that it is provided.'

I saw there was something up and at once asked what the matter was. It appears that Miss C. had told her that I had come to her and complained that she did not get the stores in properly. I thought it distinctly mean to have made my remarks, which were chiefly aimed at herself, appear as if they were a formal complaint against Miss B. I told her the real facts of the case and said I hoped she didn't think I'd be so mean as to grouse to Miss C. against her in the way Miss C. had made it appear. She was no end nice and said, no, she was sure I wouldn't, and quite accepted the olive branch, but my word, she was fearfully hurt about it at first.

Sunday, 10 October
Ever since the terrible events of 3 October, Miss B. has been too angelic for words. Took me out to tea on Cleeve Hill and done everything she possibly could for me. Even took round the milk to help me get off early. A few days ago she proposed my moving in to No. 9 as one of her boarders, and of course I jumped at it. I moved in today and I think it is going to be no end jolly. We celebrated the event by going to *A Woman of No Importance*, by Oscar Wilde. Supposed to be rather naughty, but didn't shock me at all. It's one of those modern comedy things where morals are turned upside down and laughed at, that I consider so unwholesome.

When we got home we dug out some supper from the kitchen and made cocoa before we went to bed.

Friday, 15 October
Miss B. and I decided some time ago to apply for special service with the Red Cross, which carries a salary, or some other paid post.

I can't afford to do this voluntary work much longer, nor can Miss B. I shall be very sorry indeed to leave here, but needs must, I'm afraid.

Today we were told to go to Bristol Infirmary and be interviewed by the matron. She was quite nice, but of course I was somewhat scared. Miss Yonge, the county director, told us we should be sure to be accepted as cooks are so scarce. Rather nice if we are. A screw of 20/- a week to 35/- a week, with board, and a chance of being sent to 'foreign parts'.

Well, after the interview, lunch at the Cabot, and after that, Carl Rosa's production of *Carmen*. First-rate. *Carmen* was very pretty, a splendid actress and a good voice. Then tea, and the seven o'clock home. Quite a jolly day, especially after so much spade work.

Thursday, 21 October
Home on my holiday for a fortnight. The first thing I did was to get through my medical in order to be eligible for special service. Dr G. gave me a very good report, so that part is alright anyhow. Began it by being inoculated in preparation for special services. Prepared to be very suffering, but nothing happened whatsoever except a fat arm. Miss Buckpitt is coming here for a week next Thursday, if she can find anyone to do her work at home. I do hope she comes. I think the rest will do her good. It will be very jolly having her here.

Tuesday, 26 October
Had an idea that lots of people would give things to the hospital if they knew how to get them there, so Mother and I took some sacks and baskets and a fowl crate, and put a big notice on the front of the cart and drove round Nymphsfield collecting. Up in the front we had the following notice in large red and black letters:

WHAT will you GIVE
to the Red + Hospital
Naunton Park

Potatoes	Cake	Fruit
Vegetables	Cheese	Jam
Poultry	Butter	Groceries
Rabbits	Eggs	Tea

We got heaps of things of all kinds. Only two houses refused to give. All the others fairly showered us until there was hardly any room for our little selves. Today, Sarah and I went to Uley and got rather more than

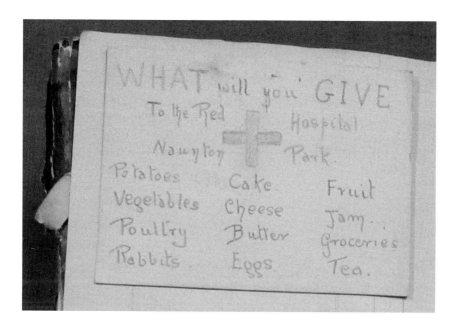

Nymphsfield. We had sacks and sacks of potatoes and vegetables, fourteen fowls, a lot of groceries and 11/- in money in the course of four days.

The Stroud Brewing Company have undertaken to drive all these provisions over to Naunton.

Wednesday, 17 November

Things are still going well at Naunton. The number of beds has been increased to 200 and we are nearly always full up. Convoys mostly arrive at 3.00 am on a Sunday or some quite preposterous hour. The unloading of the trains is done by the St John's Ambulance Brigade. They have an excellent system here, different to that in most towns. All the beds in all the hospital number 1,000. Each commandant sends to the head of the St John's Brigade a weekly report of the number of empty beds. He therefore has a list that runs something like this:

Naunton	42
St Martins	2
Racecourse	15 etc.

Each hospital has been marked down by the consulting surgeons (none of the hospitals here have resident surgeons) for some special kind of case. Thus the very small hospitals with few conveniences are only given convalescents, [and] the Red Cross wing of the General Hospital are given diseases and operation cases, because they have the experience, staff and an operating theatre. Another hospital on Cleeve Hill is given lung cases and so on.

We have the proud distinction now of having all 'tummy' cases because Naunton has got quite a reputation for its cooking. Our last consignment consisted of fifty dysentery and typhoid cases from Gallipoli. These men arrived at 1.00 am Saturday, without previous warning, and had to be fed till Monday on nothing but milk and slops, without the possibility of getting extra supplies.

We have several helpers in the kitchen. One of these is a man who, when he arrived, was deaf and dumb from shellshock. A week or two after, one of the VADs slammed the door of the ward where he was lying asleep. He woke up and swore at her, and has talked without ceasing ever since. He could give points even to Cousin Essie.

His great joy is skinning rabbits. We have fifty rabbits sent over three weeks by a neighbouring landowner, who sends to Naunton, as he thinks the cooks there are most likely to know how to cook them. On the intervening weeks, he sends a brace of pheasants or two sides of venison. With the exception of one haunch, which we had for the sisters, this is made into Irish stew. We served it the first week as venison and none of the men would touch it. We also served the roast pheasant with all the etceteras of crumbs, bread sauce etc., and the men thought the cooks had gone mad to serve 'bread and milk' with the meat, so now they go unadorned.

The dumb man has a chum who is nearly as mad as a hatter as himself. At one of the entertainments given in the central hall, these two appeared dressed as a very dashing young flapper and a young knut in civvies. How they got the clothes, I can't think. They carried on outrageously all through the concert, kissed and giggled, and giggled and tickled each other's necks and went off into little squeals and giggles. The commandant was horrified and couldn't imagine how these two horrid young people got in. I think she had half a mind to have the orderlies turn them out, only she wasn't quite sure if they would go out quietly or not.

There are three orderlies: Shadrach, Meshak and Abednego, because

they live in the midst of the fiery furnace [Daniel, chapter 3, verse 17].
'To bed we go' [Abednego] also rings the bell, puts out the lights and
locks up at bedtime

There is a certain very mangy little Cockney who has been badly
wounded in the arm. The nerve was severed. After several attempts, the
nerve has finally been successfully joined, the two ends being fastened
together with the membrane from the innards of the shell of an egg.

One of the patients was a professional singer before he joined up and
has a very fine tenor voice. He is in great demand at Cheltenham 'At
Homes' and also sings a lot in the Winter Gardens. Now and then he gives
a concert for the cooks and pantry hands, in the convalescent ward,
because we generally miss the big concerts, which are given just before
supper time.

One morning, I received a letter at my rooms addressed to Miss G.
West. It commenced with 'Darling girl' and said what a jolly time it had
been at the cinema last week, and asked if I would come again next Thurs,
and ended up 'Yours ever with lots of kisses Bob Isaacs'. The mangy little
man with the bad arm. I thought the little gentleman was trying to be very
clever at my expense, so marched up with the letter in my hand when I
next saw him and demanded what he meant by such impudence. He was
hugely tickled and went off into peals of laughter. Finally he explained
that the letter was meant for the maid. On enquiry, I found that this lady's
name is Gertie West! Now, whenever I go up to that ward with milk, I am
greeted with murmurs of 'Coming to the pictures?', 'Darling girl?',
'Yours ever with lots of kisses', and so on. Horrid, shameless little man!

In Ward 2 there are two Australians. These two were visited by a
Salvation Army lass. No. 1 entertained her, No. 2 pretended to be asleep.
When she got up to go she said, 'I should have liked to talk to your friend.'

'He's an Australian,' remarked No. 1 by way of conversation.

'Oh then, I'm afraid it is no use me leaving him any tracts is it? He
wouldn't understand the language.'

A loud guffaw came from the recumbent form of No. 2.

Tuesday, 28 December
We are just beginning to recover from Christmas festivities. I and another
girl made all the Christmas puddings, and thereby hangs a tale. Having
mixed together all the flour, currants, peel, sugar etc. in a huge bath, we
threw in the suet, which had come ready chopped from the butcher. When

we began to stir we discovered it was bad! Miss Buckpitt's wrath at our foolishness was terrible to see. She announced that the whole brew must be thrown away and that we must pay for the new ingredients as a punishment for being so stupid.

As the fruit alone cost over 30/-, this was rather terrible. After much anxious thought we devised a plan. We filled the bowl with cold water and the suet rose to the top and we skimmed it off. We then rinsed away all the wet flour and sugar and dried the fruit in the oven. We then went down to the butcher's and made him replace the bad suet gratis. All we had to pay for was the flour and the sugar, which only cost three or four shillings.

After the puddings, we made hundreds of mince pies and then a large plum cake, iced and decorated with toy saucepans and kettles, as this was to be a present from the cooks to the Tommies.

Turkey, pudding and cake.

There was some anxiety as to how to raise enough turkey for 250 people. But Miss Buckpitt put an advert in the local paper asking who would like to give a turkey to Naunton Park. We got sixteen, most of them immense, and kept the eight biggest. The others we graciously bestowed on other hospitals. They weren't grateful; on the contrary, rather annoyed not to have thought of it themselves and thinking of our having enough to give away, while they were having to eke out with mere roast beef.

Of course, we had roast potatoes, greens, sausages, stuffing and all the other fixings. Quantities of fruit, crackers and sweets were given by various people and six or eight iced cakes, including one monster 2½ feet across, from the doctors who offered it as a prize to the best decorated ward.

The decorations were wonderfully good. One or two were just decked out with a medley of gaudy papers, but most were most carefully designed. One inhabited by several Welshmen was entirely decorated in daffodils and yellow and green paper. Another consisted of cotton wool snow, holly, mistletoe, robins etc. Another, the prize-winner, was a Japanese design, peach blossom, fans and so on, and the men all wore kimonos.

We had concerts, entertainments and dances galore. Now we are feeling rather flat and very feeble, but it was a great success. I am sure lots of the men never had such a jolly Xmas before.

One of them sent a message: 'To the cook who did the plum pudding that he would be pleased to marry her only unfortunately he'd got a wife already.'

This poster shows women working at a lathe in a factory. It was published in 1915 to raise money for the Women's War Time Fund to provide rest rooms, canteens and hostels for women doing war work.
Library of Congress

1916

Saturday, 1 January

We have heard no more from the Red Cross Society. I cannot afford to stay on much longer in a voluntary job. Miss B. has also been seeking a paid post, so she and I have decided to accept the offer of Lady Lawrence's Canteen Committee to put us in charge of a canteen for girls at the Royal Aircraft Factory, Farnborough, Hampshire. Miss B. goes tomorrow and I follow a few days later. So, goodbye Naunton. I shall be very sorry to leave, but needs must. I can't afford to be voluntary any more.

Friday, 7 January

Tomorrow I am off to my new job as cook at a canteen in Farnborough. I am to have a salary of £60 a year and two meals a day, and am to cook for about 250 of the girls at the Royal Aircraft Factory. The canteen is being run by a committee in London – The Munition Makers Canteen Committee. Miss Buckpitt is to be their travelling organizer going about from place to place starting canteens, and to inspect them and keep them up to the mark when started. She is to start operations at Farnborough, so at any rate, for a few weeks we shall be together. She went there a few days ago to interview trades people and beat up voluntary helpers. I am to meet her there tomorrow and the canteen opens Monday, so we shall have a busy weekend.

Saturday, 8 January

Not a very cheerful outlook when I first arrived. Miss B. was to have met me at the station, but was not there, and by some mistake I eventually got out at North Camp instead of South Farnborough, so that was a nice 2 miles to bicycle to our lodgings. I had with me a despatch case, fibre trunk, camp bed, mattress and a hamper, also Rip. I had to leave all except Rip and the despatch case and arrange for the rest to be returned to South Farnborough. Did a melancholy 3 miles peddling through the mud, with Rip tailing disconsolately behind. Several airplanes flew low across the road, and each time Rip squatted flat in the road petrified and refused to come on. As the road was full of traffic, it gave me several bad spasms.

At last I arrived at 'Ye Olde Farm House', as it is called, and was told Miss B. had not been able to meet me, but would I go down to the factory to see her. So I splashed back to the factory. Here I was met at the gates by an armed sentry who refused flatly to let me in. I went round to the other gate and was held up by a policeman. Returned to first gate and found a baker's cart also trying frantically to get to 'the new canteen'.

Ye Olde Farm House.

We were told there was no new canteen, and we ought to have passes and he wasn't going to let strange people into the factory etc. However, by the simple process of just 'remaining' until he got tired of the look of us, we were let in.

Then I had to find the canteen. No one had ever heard of it and it was rather like hunting a needle in a haystack – you are told it is near the head office and you find they are talking of the men's canteen. Then you are told to turn left when you get to the oil store and you have to find out which is the oil store. Then you are told, 'It's no good going that way, the mud is too deep, you'd better go round by V department and then down

The sleeper road to the machine shop.

the sleeper road till you get to the machine shop etc. Well, after a bit I arrived at the end of a long series of planks, which led across a huge morass to a wee little wooden hut, but there was no Miss Buckpitt, so I had to go away and come back later.

This time I found a very forlorn looking figure sitting on a box in the empty canteen, no table, no chairs, pots or pans, no cupboards or shelves, only three tiny gas stoves, Miss Buckpitt and the box, and at the far end, two men slowly and solemnly washing the floor. They had only one bucket, one piece of soap and one flannel between them so their progress was not exactly rapid.

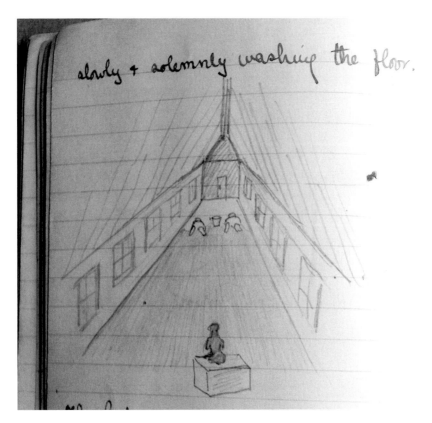

Miss Buckpitt and the floor washers.

The equipment was supposed to be on the road, so we sat and waited for its arrival. It turned up at about 7.30 and we worked like slaves the rest of the evening till nearly ten, unpacking and putting it in order. As the canteen was to open on Monday, there wasn't much time to waste.

Sunday, 9 January
Was spent at the canteen cooking and otherwise preparing to astonish the world on Monday. The two men turned up again and continued to slowly wash the floor. Two more brought tables and chairs, and two more began laying linoleum. Then a carpenter turned up and began making cupboards and shelves, so that by about nine o'clock, what had been a bare and empty barrack had turned into quite a plausible kitchen and mess room.

Farnborough itself is a beastly place. It consists of one long ribbon of mud designated 'the main road'. At one end are the shops, at the other are our rooms, and about halfway between, the factory. The shops don't bear talking about. They look about on a par with those at Nailsworth. In reality, they are not even in the same street with them. At Nailsworth, if you enter a shop they at any rate express a mild and passing interest in you and your requirements. At Farnborough, you go in feeling rather important. You announce you belong to the 'Girls' canteen RAF': that you would like to hear a quote for a large order. You rather expect a bowing manager anxious to obey your behests. On the contrary; you are confronted by a small girl or possibly a youth who looks you up and down and answers coldly, 'We are not taking on any new orders now, but perhaps we could oblige you.' Reductions? 'Oh, I am afraid we can't make any reduction on our current price.' When can we deliver? 'Oh, hardly know, but daresay we might if you give us several days' notice. Wouldn't suit? Sorry, good afternoon.' By the time you have spent a whole morning at this you want to strafe the lot.

The rooms are a different matter. They are in a very old house, which was once a farm. 'Ye Olde Farm House'. A delightful sitting room with French windows into the garden and a private staircase leading to a huge double bedroom, and for Farnborough very cheap, only 18/-, whereas many people are paying £2 or even 3 guineas for worse. The only disadvantage is that they are about 2 miles from the factory.

The country round is very pretty – pine trees, heather and rhododendrons, rather like Bournemouth – but the roads are perfectly vile, cut to bits by the motor transport wagons. Also, large tracts of country are covered by barracks, ranges, etc., so that if one does not know one's way, one may walk for miles through about a foot of mud in the most desolate country, nothing but gas works, waste land and army buildings. But to anyone not used to it, the flying and the soldiers are most exciting. There are nearly always from two to ten to twelve aeroplanes up, some of them looping the loop, doing the most wonderful spirals, banking etc. Sometimes they swing first their 'heads' up and then their 'tails' up, then go along in waves, or shoot straight up and come down in a spiral, so straight that the inside wing is over practically the same spot all the time. We once started to walk across a large flat field when an aeroplane landed and began scuttling straight for us – my word, did we run. Being chased by a bull is bad, but an aeroplane is ten times the size and had six times the pace; it's horrid!

The procession.

On the Aldershot road there is a continual procession of soldiers – first a train of mule wagons, then a military band, then twenty or thirty guns, each drawn by six horses, then a detachment of cavalry, then horses out for exercise, then a little squad of flying corps men, then a string of motor transports, then a whole camp moving quarters, baggage wagons, field kitchens, and all the rest of it – frightfully exciting.

Monday, 10 January

Our first day at canteen work. Found that there was hardly any gas pressure, so that it took hours to get the potatoes to boil, and it seemed almost impossible to get the meat to roast. And if you light more than two of the five comic little stoves, they all go out. However, things did get done somehow, but we only sold about six plates of meat and no pudding. At tea we had rather more to do, but not a great deal, but still, we don't feel a bit discouraged. Naturally they sent out scouts at first to spy out the land, and if they only take back a favourable report, I hope the others will soon follow.

Tuesday, 11 January

Sold about twenty dinners today, so we are getting on. Our menu is something after this style:

Monday		and	Tuesday	
Roast Mutton	6d		Roast Beef	6d
potatoes			carrots	
cabbage			potatoes	
Irish Stew	5d		Meat pasties	3d
Rice Pudding	2d		Spotted Dick	2d

We shall go in for more elaborations later, but with the gas so bad, can't do anything very ambitious.

Friday, 14 January

Most of the girls are quite nice and quite quiet. We have about a dozen clerks who come down before the general dinner hour. They are rather haughty, but not so bad. The others are ordinary factory girls from various departments of the factory. There are the 'Welders', who join the metal parts of the planes by means of strong acetylene blow lamps. These give out such dazzling sparks and flames that they have to wear dark blue, almost black, goggles. They also wear blue linen overalls and caps.

Then there are the 'dope' girls. They varnish the planes with fast-drying, very poisonous varnish. It affects the liver, therefore the girls thus employed are under medical supervision, have to drink large quantities

Women workers sitting down for a meal in the canteen of a British munitions factory.
WWI 1914–1918 British Press photograph collection / UBC Library

of lime juice and lemonade, must not eat in the dope room, must wash before meals etc.

But the majority are 'Cody's girls'. Mr Cody is the foreman of the 'shop' where the planes are covered with linen. He is the son of the Cody who invented the biplane and was eventually killed in an aeroplane accident. His uncle was Buffalo Bill. He is an awful little bounder but quite amiable.

There is one girl, and luckily only one, who is the most accomplished little cheat I have ever met. Nearly every day she devises some new scheme for 'doing us down', and as the voluntary workers are constantly changing and some of them are not over bright in any case, she very often succeeds.

The first time she gave me 1/- or half a crown for a 1d cup of tea, received change from one worker, went away and presently came back to another worker and vowed she'd not yet been given her change. Next day she gave me seven halfpennies for something worth 4d – in the scrimmage of serving dinners it very nearly got overlooked. When this no longer worked she devised the plan of buying a cup of tea, carrying it to a distant table and coming back would ask for the loan of the milk jug a minute as the tea was so hot. Then she drinks the tea, refills the cup with milk and returns the half-empty jug, at no charge. Of course, no one but these silly old volunteers would allow the milk to be carted off this way. She really is so ingenious; I can't help having a sneaking admiration for her.

Monday, 17 January
Really, voluntary workers are the limit. About eight out of ten are married women and yet there is only one out of the whole lot who knows the barest elements of cookery and housekeeping, and there are not more than half a dozen with even a glimmer of commonsense. Yesterday I asked one of them to peel the potatoes and was immediately bombarded with the following list of questions:

1. How many?
2. Where are they?
3. What shall I do them with?
4. What do I put them in?
5. Do I peel them in hot water or cold?
6. Where shall I put the peelings?

Now I admit that question 1 was reasonable, but I should have thought any child knew the answers to numbers 3 and 5. As to the remaining three questions, I may remark that the potatoes are kept in a sack in the scullery, there are four or five buckets beside the sink and there is a refuse tub just outside the door.

There are two very dashing young ladies who come sometimes; they are covered with paint and powder and smoke cigarettes etc. I set them to peel potatoes and onions and they were frightfully delighted, attacked the job with shrieks and chuckles of glee. I remarked to one of the other workers that they seemed to be having a high time over it and she smiled and remarked, 'Well you see, I don't suppose they have ever done that sort of job before. They are the nieces of the Duchess of Wellington.'

Another of the good ladies is the most typical Sunday school teacher you ever saw, pale and colourless and dull, very self-satisfied and virtuous, and I should say, not more than two ideas in her head. She always goes by the name of 'Teacher' or 'MaryAnn'. She must be one of the happiest beings in creation, so entirely pleased with herself and conscious of her own righteousness.

Saturday, 22 January

The factory is a huge place – all quite new, and is built almost entirely of corrugated iron. There are two huge sheds, which once held the two dirigibles, *Alpha* and *Beta*, but they have gone to glory and the sheds have been turned into stores.

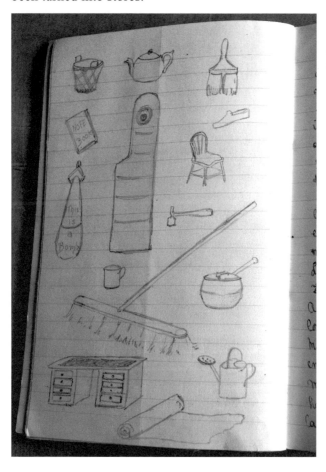

Items from Mr Cooper's stores.

The stores are quite wonderful. Mr Cooper, the head thereof, can supply you with any mortal thing. William Whiteley [founder of Whiteleys department store] isn't in the running with him. He keeps furniture, linen, silk, felt slippers, nuts, screws, steel, iron, aluminium, varnish, aeroplane wings, engines, motor bikes, stationary, brooms, kettles, dustpans, mirrors, whitewash, paint brushes, brooms, trolleys, paper baskets, mats, chamois leathers, teapots, safes, cupboards, and a hundred other things. Anything we haven't got at the canteen we ask him for and it promptly arrives, from chopping boards and meat safes down to sanitary dustbins, from lemon squeezers to linoleum.

Wednesday, 26 January
The Committee have announced that they wish Miss Buckpitt to go to Woolwich at the end of the month, where they are about to open a very big new canteen. I am to stay on at Farnborough. I am to be cook caterer and another lady is to do the financial part, i.e. count the money, pay the bills etc.

Rather an awkward sort of position for me as, of course, that means I shall be in reality responsible for the success or otherwise of the show, because although she will pay the bills, yet I shall get blamed, being caterer, if they are too high, and also I shall get blamed if the food is not to their liking, being cook.

I am frightfully scared, very near a blue panic, in fact, and also don't know how I shall endure being only myself in digs. Miss B. is such a ripping person to live with, although she is a good deal older than I am and also is my 'boss' during working hours. She never slacks or shirks the various little jobs at home. In fact, she does a great deal more than her fair share in the way of bed making, laying and cooking the meals etc. You see, we do all that part for ourselves, as we do not pay our landlady for attendance.

And Miss B. is also one of the most delightful people to go out. She is just like you [Gabrielle's brother Michael] in that she is always game for a lark and quite ready to sally forth in search of adventure whenever we get a chance of a little time off.

Sunday, 30 January
Miss B. has just settled up the first month's bills. The takings and the current expenses just balance, but there is nothing over to go towards the

initial outlay and we have got between £30 and £40 to pay off, which was advanced by the London Committee for equipment etc. Still, it is very good for the first month, when everything had to be bought and there is nothing in hand. But next month, of course, it ought to begin to pay its way; I only hope it will. I shall live in terror of Feb 29th from now on.

Tuesday, 1 February

Miss B. left this morning and so I am feeling very scared during work hours and very lonesome during free time, so at present I am not leading at all a happy life.

Mrs Bradley, my partner, seems quite nice, not very energetic and a rather rude blasé manner. She is quite young, not more than about two years older than myself, and has a husband at the front. Whether she will be what you might call an enthusiastic worker or not, I don't know.

The Committee have sent down another lady who is also anxious to take rooms in the place and work in the canteen. She is a young war widow, rather pretty, languid, fashionable, very pleasant, and quite a good sort. But she is very delicate and very lacking in vitality, and doesn't know a boiled egg from a turnip.

Monday, 14 February

Just come back from the factory. I spent Saturday and Sunday in town with Miss Buckpitt. She has not begun to work at Woolwich yet. Has only been down to prospect and is now in London buying equipment.

I arrived Saturday afternoon and met her at the Munition Makers' Canteen Committee office in Victoria Street, and then we went to tea and afterwards to *Tales of Hoffman* [the Offenbach opera], at the Shaftesbury. Quite good but not a very interesting plot, and the voices were not very special either. Not up to *Carmen*.

Afterwards we had supper at a little place just opposite and went back to our rooms. Next day, went to Westminster Abbey, then to Soho to eat sticky buns, then to see a canteen worker at Camden Hill, and then back again to Soho, where we had a 1/6d at one of those the little foreign restaurants. Miss B. was frightfully fascinated; it was her initiation into the excitements of Bohemia. I don't think she had even heard of the 'Petit Riche' and 'Brise' or Old Compton Street before, and the horse butcher and sausage shops nearly gave her fits.

She seems to have had the most entertaining time at Woolwich. She went down to inspect the scene of her labour. The canteen exists already, but is only doing a few teas. Her job is to start it doing 500 dinners.

Apparently, the London Committee had quite forgotten to write and introduce her, for when she arrived she was taken for an ordinary voluntary and set down to 'put out buns'. Then she was told she had done that quite nicely, and did she know how to use a bread cutting machine? She said she thought so, so was set to cut bread and butter. After this the girls began to come for tea and she sold buns and oranges industriously.

One of the girls asked her when the dinners would begin and she replied, 'Oh, next week, I hope.' Whereupon the lady next to her remarked severely, 'How do you know? You've only just come.' Miss B. felt crushed. Then she was told she might go; she remarked she would soon be coming back but was tired.

'Oh well, we don't need any new helpers just now, so please don't trouble to come until we send for you. Perhaps later on we might be able to fit you in.'

They'll feel rather flat when they find what sort of an angel they have entertained unawares.

We are kept pretty cheerful here with Zeppelin scares. Every now and then the lights in the factory are all turned off and all the soldiers called out by the hooter etc., and then next morning we hear there has been a raid on the East Coast or some equally remote spot. The other night, the lights in the canteen suddenly went out. Of course, we all thought it was a Zeppelin again and sat patiently waiting for a bomb to alight on our heads. However, after about an hour we woke up to the fact that all the rest of the factory was lit up as usual, so it gradually dawned on us that it was merely something wrong with our wires, and that it was about time we went and bullied the electrician about it.

Tuesday, 22 February
Mother and Father arrived today. They had been up in London, where Father lectured at the Royal Institute. They first came to the canteen, where I regaled them with a 6d dinner. Then we went all over the factory. Of course, you are not supposed to go prying around, but we managed it, with a little subterfuge. We started with Mr Cooper and went all over the stores dept. Then from him we got the name of the boss of the machine shop. We then trotted across to the machine shop and said, 'Mr Cooper said he thought Mr Hall would not mind us seeing his shop.'

Mr Hall was of course quite charmed. From him we got the name of the boss of the next shop, and so on right through. A great deal of it is just like any other factory; just rows of machines, circular saws etc., so that part where the girls cover the planes is the most interesting.

First of all the linen is passed over a glass-topped table, with a kind of green tent over it and a powerful electric light under the glass. In this way, any little hole or weak spot is detected and marked. After this the holes are 'patched', that is a little square of stuff with frazzled-out edges is pasted over them. If there is the least fault in the linen of a plane, there is the danger that the wind whistling through it may make it tear right across.

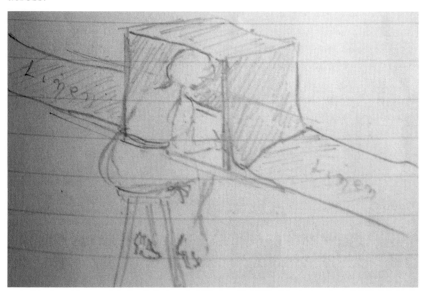

The glass-topped table and green tent used to inspect the fabric.

Then the plane is covered with linen in a very neat and clever sort of way. Then it is 'doped', or varnished, all over, three or four times in succession. This makes the linen taut like parchment, and also waterproof. After this they are painted and sent over to another shed to be fixed to the bodies. Some of these pieces are huge things, though when on the aeroplanes they do not appear so. The largest measure 30ft each, making the aeroplane, counting the breadth of the body, measure 70ft across from tip to tip of the planes.

When we got home I found a letter from Miss Buckpitt saying she was coming for two nights, on Thursday. Fearful consternation as Mother is in her bed, and was intending to stay till Tues. So of course, as we couldn't turn her out of her own bed, poor mother had to move into a cottage nearby, where after much searching we managed to find her a bed.

Saturday, 26 February

Miss B. and I went down to inspect the new canteen that is being built for us. Our present place is much too small and only a temporary affair. The new one is quite a palace and is to be no end smart when finished, with all the latest improvements, but of course, it isn't very far advanced as yet, so there wasn't a great deal to see. The little man who showed us round was rather rude and tried to be very snubbing when Miss B. suggested any improvements. At last, she remarked that she had so much experience of manmade kitchens it had made her a little wary. He was frightfully indignant and said he was quite sure there would be nothing wrong with a kitchen of his design. I remarked mildly, 'Well, Mr Metcalf, how would you like it if I designed your machine shop?'

'Not at all,' he said very rudely. 'Well,' said I quite sweetly, 'now you know how we feel when we hear you are going to design us a kitchen. Everyone to his own job, you know.' He looked so savage, poor dear.

Monday, 28 February

Poor Mother had to go home suddenly as Father has fallen off the study steps and hurt himself rather badly. It was very sad as we had such a jolly week. Mother came down three times and helped with the cooking, and it really was a joy to get someone who did know what they were playing at.

Wednesday, 1 March

Just finished the month's accounts. Out of £56 takings, we have paid out £8 5s in salaries, £8 4s in materials, and made a clear profit of £14. That is really very good as it means a profit of 25 per cent, so I feel rather bucked. Although these canteens are started by society ladies as a sort of contribution to the war, they are not supposed to be charities, but are expected to pay back the money advanced for equipment, and after that to make enough so that when the war ends they can be kept on with paid instead of voluntary help. Any extra profits will be put to charitable uses.

A very good scheme, I consider. Much better than pauperizing people who are earning record wages and are quite able to pay fair prices for good value.

Made another desperate attempt to go for a country walk. This time I started out to Bagshot Heath. The road was ankle-deep in mud, fearful soupy stuff. On each side were barracks and stretches of mud dugouts and trenches. Every now and then you come on a row of ghastly 'corpses' swinging in the wind, awful bloated sacks with straw sticking out of the 'bayonet wounds'.

'Corpses', swinging in the wind.

Every few yards, a wagon or motor transport passed and spattered mud right up to one's neck. All the time there was a thin drizzle falling, so it was thoroughly jolly and festive.

Rip pattered along at my heels, grunting and puffing with rage when he got splashed or met with an extra formidable puddle. We paddled along like this for about 5 miles, getting more and more depressed until at last we got to Chobham Ridges, which is really quite interesting. From there we went into a corner of Bagshot Heath.

Neither is at its best in winter, being rather black and dismal, but it is quite romantic. Miles of peat and heather and dead bracken, with a few pine trees and gorse bushes, and little peaty streams running amongst them. In the mist and wind and drizzle it made me think of Beau Brocade and Dick Turpin, and all the tales of people robbed and murdered, and highwaymen hung in chains and creaking corpses in the wind.

But 5 miles through mud in a drizzle isn't very inspiring. Quite refreshing, after the deadly monotony of Farnborough.

Monday, 13 March
Miss Buckpitt arrived suddenly today. Much to my amazement, the Committee sent her down to ask me if I would accept the job of caterer to the new canteen at Woolwich. There are various points in its favour. In the first place, I am very dull at Farnborough, and as Miss B. is to be at least four months at Woolwich so as to open seven new canteens, I shall see a good deal of her if I go there. Then there is to be a rise from 25/- a week to 34/-, which will make all the difference. 25/- is a fearful squeeze when rooms and laundry and everything else is so dear. Thirdly, it is a distinct promotion, as Woolwich is a much larger canteen than Farnborough. So I have accepted and am to go on Mon next if I can succeed in persuading my 'partner', Mrs Bradley, to take over Farnborough and get a paid cook to help her.

Saturday, 18 March
A day or two ago I got a letter from Miss Buckpitt saying that the Committee had changed their plans and were writing. However, as they didn't write, and as I had squared Mrs Bradley and installed the cook, I determined to make tracks for Woolwich before they had a chance to stop me. So I bolted off to London today and am staying till Monday with Charlie [brother], after which I go to Woolwich. I took care not to leave any address: don't want to receive their old letter if I can avoid it.

Tuesday, 21 March
Gave Miss B. frightful shocks by marching in upon her yesterday. The Committee apparently decided that Farnborough couldn't exist without me and wrote to put me off. How I managed to miss the letter I can't think! Anyway, Miss B. went to London today and told the Committee that I was here and very put out at being made a fool of in this way, and wasn't going back to Farnborough at any price. So they meekly climbed down and I am now to be night head at Woolwich. I begin my duties tonight, which means twenty-four hours out of bed, worse luck.

Wednesday, 22 March

Quite enjoyed myself last night, in spite of being very sleepy. There is a lot to do all the time. The boys are in and out all the time, buying cakes and tea and lemonade etc. At 11.30, a big batch of girls come to dinner. It is really immensely more exciting than Farnborough.

As for Woolwich, it is of course a slummy part of London. In fact, there are slums all the way between here and London, which is one and a half hours by tram. But it is rather amusing for all that. Beresford Square, outside the main gate, is a big market full of coster's barrows, fruit, vegetables, fish, tripe, winkles, flowers, knives and tools, livestock and all the various wares you see at Petticoat Lane. There are also street jugglers, palmists, etc. performing.

All along the road to the Arsenal are weird little shops, rather like the North End Road [this is in Hammersmith, West London, and to this day has a market].

There is also a sort of crèche for pipes and baccy. The work people are not allowed to take their smoking outfit into the Arsenal, so for a few pence a week they can leave them just outside the gate. There are four gates, each one about a mile and a half from the next, and after reaching the third gate, which is the one we go in at, we still have a good twenty-five minutes' walk. Imagine Oxford Street with no pavements and no islands, but with a railway running down each side, and the road a sea of mud and rubbish, and you will have an idea of what the 'Long Straight' at Woolwich is like.

You leap out of the way of a motor lorry and land under a train, bundle out from there and run full tilt into a swearing navvy who wants to know, by all that's holy, [why] you can't look where you are going. It's the limit.

The canteen is between the danger buildings and the firing pits, so by day the noise from the guns is tremendous, cups leap off the shelves and every now and again a window breaks, but luckily I am spared that at night.

We serve a lot of boys with buns, sweets, oranges, tea, mineral waters etc. all through the night, also a few men. Then we give dinners to a lot of girls and some men at 11.30. At 3.30, tea for the girls, at 4.00, tea for the boys, at 5.30, more boys and a lot of men, so we are busy the whole night except 12.30–3.00, when we have our own meal, scrub all the tables etc. It is pretty strenuous; far more exciting than Farnborough!

We take from £4 to £5 every night, and by day they get £12–£15.

When you remember that nearly all of it comes in in coppers [pennies, ha'pennies and farthings], it means a good deal of work.

The girls are very rough, regular Cockneys, but mostly very nice and amiable, but if one does happen to get roused, it is just Billingsgate gone mad. If they are aggressive the only thing is to be equally so and to give them as good as you get; they generally shut up and become quite meek when they see you are unabashed by their abuse. One of them attacked me today because she had to wait a minute or two for her dinner. We were short of helpers and were going as hard as ever we could, so I whipped round and said, 'Well, how many pairs of hands do you think I've got? Six?' She looked quite abashed and shut up at once.

Some of them come from the fuse shop, but a good many from the danger buildings. This is where they fill the cartridges etc. for bombs. They have no end of rules and regulations. When they arrive they have to go to a barrier, take off their shoes, jump over the barrier in stocking feet and put on slippers on the other side, for fear of any grit coming in on their shoes. They also are not allowed any hairpins, so wear their hair down their backs in plaits, and also they must not wear any metal buttons etc. on their clothes. Their work is chiefly filling the cartridge cases for bombs.

The workmen who work in the further parts of the factory go to work on the weirdest little trains with wee little engines and trucks like the Irish jaunting cars. When four or five trucks are strung together it is most comic

The men sitting side by side on the train.

to see a long row of men, each with his red handkerchief on his knees, sitting side by side like a long row of swallows on a telegraph wire, or more like old hens on a perch.

Saturday, 1 April

A frightful thrill; have been through an air raid! I must give you a full and solemn account of the whole performance. As I came to work at about 8.00 pm I met a whole lot of the gunners going along the same way. I said I was surprised to see them going to work at such an hour, as all the gun testing is done by day. They smiled and said they thought they were going to do a little tonight. I remarked that I wanted to know what happened to the shells; didn't they fly for miles and do damage, or did they only use a sort of blank charge? Whereupon they sniggered and said they thought they might be using real shells tonight, but even then I never realized that they were out after Zeps.

We had not been long in the canteen before the foreman of the bandoleer shop came butting around adjusting the curtains etc., and it began to dawn on me that we were in for a raid.

'I'll send some of the boys over to get something to eat,' he remarked., so for about twenty minutes we were busy serving buns, tea, coffee, mineral waters etc.

Just as the last boy was served, out went the lights. As soon as the lights go out, each foreman is supposed to lock the door of his shop. This is a necessary precaution because one could not have hundreds of panicky men and women charging about in the dark in the open.

However, we were not locked in, though we had a watchman standing at one door and the foreman at the other, which opens into the bandolier shop. Some of the girls in the shops near started to squeal and then began to sing, but the boys were absolutely quiet. There wasn't a sound except the policemen whistling to each other and the foreman and watchman calling 'Are you there Tom?' 'Yes, George.'

Then all of a sudden, the guns began. They don't make a great noise, only a sharp, short bang, almost like revolver shot. Of course, the big naval guns make a deafening noise, but they did not fire them tonight.

I made tracks for the door in hope of seeing. The Zep was just about 3 miles up, like a small sausage in the sky, very high up. The minute it came into sight, three searchlights were playing on it and the guns opened fire. It was hit three times. Each time it lurched and then gave a bound.

Then it rose higher still in the air, turned round and did an ignominious bolt. The whole performance was over in five minutes.

As the Zep retreated it began dropping bombs. These landed partly in the river, one or two in North Woolwich, where they destroyed two or three small houses and killed several people, and the rest in fields and open ground, where no damage was done.

Obviously the Zep was badly hit, as she came down very low and seemed lopsided as she disappeared and made an effort to get home before she collapsed, but failed, for in the morning there was great rejoicing at the news that she had come down in the Thames.

Meanwhile, we sat in darkness. It got very cold, as the radiators were turned off, so we lit the ovens and sat in front of them with the doors open. There were only four of us, the cook, the char, the old watchman and myself. The watchman is the weirdest old bird. The very fattest, stupidest old thing you ever saw. He is exactly like a tortoise; he has not only got the face of one, but also the figure, and just about the brain power. He talks in slow gasps, with long wheezing pauses between, like an old person who has just woken out of a nightmare, and he often spends the whole night from 7.00 pm to 6.00 am asleep in front of the radiator, except that he occasionally rouses himself sufficiently to eat a little food in the torpid sort of way that a tortoise eats dandelions.

I suppose he thought it was his duty to try to cheer and encourage us poor females, so he roused himself from his hibernation and remarked, 'Last time we had a raid, I did have a dreadful time, I did. When the lights went out, the cook was here and "Oh," she says, "you wicked man," she sez, "to turn out the light," she sez. "You wicked man." And she takes hold of my coat, she does, and I thought she would have hit me she looked so savage. And the char woman there! She hung on to my arm and cry! My word did she cry! And I says to them, "My good women," I sez, "it ain't my fault," I sez, but it wasn't a bit of use; they kept on just the same.'

The thought of that poor old reptile besieged on one side by a frantic cook and on the other by a tearful char was so funny that I simply roared, until the tortoise slowly turned his head towards me and remarked, 'Zepperlins weren't no laughing matter in his opinion.'

After that, I felt rebuked and subsided. After this, he regaled us with spicy reminiscences of the wreck of the *Princess Alice (*a pleasure steamer that was rammed and went down with all on board somewhere near here).

He especially dwelt on the rows of corpses in the mortuary and other pleasing aspects of the tragedy. It all happened thirty years ago.

Well, we managed to while away the rest of the night fairly comfortably, what with frequent meals and long snoozes, and the *Princess Alice*, until about 3.30. The lights came up again, and in five minutes, in came a whole hoard of girls, men and boys, all clamouring for dinner. Of course, none of the volunteers had turned up so I and the cook had to do everything, with the char in the background. Luckily, the boiled beef and carrots were cooking before the lights went out, but there was of course no pudding. Most of the girls were quite nice and reasonable and waited patiently till we could serve them, but one remarked very aggressively, 'I've been waiting quite five minutes for my dinner.' The girl next to her turned round and said, 'Don't be so unreasonable. You ought to be jolly thankful you've got an inside left to put your dinner in, you little beast.' She subsided very suddenly.

Monday, 3 April

Another Zep scare, and another six hours in the dark, but this time the Zep didn't come anywhere very near, though we heard guns going about 6 miles away.

You should see my respirator. We were each given one on Saturday in case the Zep dropped asphyxiating bombs, and the watchman forgot to ask for mine back. Nasty little black gauze things. I found out after that they are no use unless wetted. As they were given out in little oil-silk parcels in the pitch dark, I don't suppose anyone could have found their way into them in time even if the Zep had dropped any numbers of 'stink bombs'. I am frightfully proud of mine. Fancy having a real live respirator!

Thursday, 6 April

Have been to London to interview various members of the Committee. Miss Rathbone, whose pet canteen is Farnborough. She wanted to know if I would go back there. I said no, it wasn't large enough to give scope for my great abilities. She said she was very grieved, and in that case would I go and talk to Miss Fry, but she wanted to see me first in case I was willing to return to the Aircraft Factory. Well, then I saw Miss Fry. Her pets are three canteens at Abbey Wood, about 2 miles beyond Woolwich. No. 1 is quite old and has been jogging along for about two

106

years. No. 2 canteen started in December to cater for fifty-two girls, and now has to deal with 600. The volunteer lady superintendent has lost grip of it and wants to get married, so is leaving. No. 3 is new and is to be opened by Miss Buckpitt in two or three days. Miss Fry wanted to know if I would take the management of No. 2. I said I would prefer to keep at Woolwich, either as day or night head. She said she was afraid that this wasn't possible, so eventually I said I would take on No. 2 for a month on trial if they would raise my screw to 34/- instead of 25/- a week. This was agreed; they meekly acquiesced, so I am to start on the 10th so as to be a week with the old head before starting on my own.

Saturday, 8 April
There is such a quaint old gentleman here. He brought me a bunch of flowers the other day when he came for his dinner and began telling me how he lived all alone except for his 'old girl' and his garden. The old girl comes to the tramway halt every night to meet him. I thought, what a very dutiful wife. Later, he asked me for a few bones for the 'old girl'. She turns out to be an Airedale, not a wife. So he brings me the most beautiful dahlias, Michaelmas daisies and roses, and I give him in return the most succulent bones and broken cakes.

The stoker is also rather an oddity. He has a great admiration for Rip, who always comes to work with me. He gives him a bath every month in the boiler house. Rip loathes the sight of him in consequence.

Three men in the neighbouring shop also admire Rip. They bring him traps full of rats to kill. When he arrives in the morning, the first thing he does is to rush off to these three to see if there is anything doing in the rat line. If there are none in the traps, the four go off on the hunt and poke out the holes, turn over the boxes etc. while Rip kills any rats that run out.

The engineer's assistant has the most marvellous appetite. I cook his breakfast every morning. Yesterday there were four sausages and a gammon rasher weighing half a pound. I weighed it out of curiosity. No wonder they say £5 a week isn't enough to live on. In return for cooking the breakfasts he brings me presents of chocolate, and very nice too.

Rip has had several adventures in the Arsenal. Dogs are not allowed inside, as a matter of fact. But the police at the gate have always winked the other eye at Rip. But a few weeks ago, a new and very aggressive young man arrived – informed me the first morning, 'Dogs are not allowed inside the Arsenal.' I said, 'I know that,' and trotted on. Next day, he told me the same thing and I told him very sweetly that this was a special dog. Next day, I went in at a different gate and to my great disgust encountered the enemy again, who told me that if he found the dog again he should refuse to let us in. So I went off to the Assistant Lady Super, Lady Lindsay, who has a photo of a dog pinned up in her office. This made me think I might get a sympathetic audience in her. She rose to the occasion nobly. Next day, I received a pass signed by the Arsenal Superintendent – 'Admit Miss West's dog Rip' – for the purpose of preparing meals for munitions workers. (This pass must be carried by the person in whose name it is drawn out.)

Next day, Rip trotted in with the pass in his mouth. He must be the only dog that ever received a government pass.

Rip's Pass

The pass still exists, in the diary in the Imperial War Museum, London. It is a small piece of ordinary paper that states:

ROYAL ORDNANCE FACTORIES
The bearer Miss West's dog Rip
has permission to proceed to
Inspection Dept Dining Rooms
in order to assist in the
provision of Meals for
Munition Workers
Ast Sec
for Actg. Chief Superintendent
of Ordnance Factories
3/8/1916
N.B. This pass is not
transferable and must be
produced when demanded by the
POLICE or any other responsible person acting on behalf
of the site C.S.O.F

The diary went to India, and Bobby's brother Michael sent the story to an unknown Indian newspaper. In the course of time, the cutting came home. It too is in the diary, much degraded, and relates:

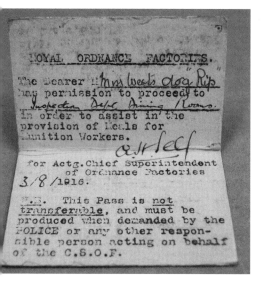

RIP AND HIS PASS
A DOG MUNITION WORKER

The following amusing incident is related in a letter received by a resident of Calcutta, from his sister who is managing the workers' canteen at one of the largest Government munition works in England. She writes:–

Of late a new policeman has appeared at _____ and the beast started a regular feud against Rip. Dogs aren't allowed in the works but all the other police constables look the other way.

Well, for about a week he raised a fuss every morning. At last he said 'Now Miss, don't you bring that dog in again because I won't let him in.' So I went in by another gate and to my horror met my old enemy again. I began to get desperate, but next time I saw Lady L____, the Welfare Superintendant, who inspects our canteens, I asked her if she could get Rip a pass. She said she'd try and in due course arrived a proper pass, signed by one of the big pots, which solemnly set forth:-

RIP AND HIS PASS.

A DOG MUNITION WORKER.

THE following amusing incident is related in a letter received by a resident of Calcutta from his sister, who is managing the workers' canteen at one of the largest Government munition works in England. She writes:—

Of late a new policeman has appeared at —— and the beast started a regular feud against Rip. Dogs aren't allowed in the works, but all the other police constables discreetly look the other way. Well, for about a week he raised a fuss every morning. At last he said " Now Miss, don't you bring that dog again, because I won't let him in." So I went in by another gate and to my horror met my old enemy again. I began to get desperate, but next time I saw Lady L——, the Welfare Superintendent, who inspects our canteens, I asked her if she could get Rip a pass. She said she'd try and in due course arrived a proper pass, signed by one of the big pots, which solemnly sets forth:

Please admit:—
Name—"Rip" Miss W.'s dog.
Destination—E 34 a.
Business—To assist in the preparation of meals for munition workers.
Note.—This pass is not transferable. Bearer must produce the same when required, and answer all questions put by the police or other persons in authority.

Since then I've been busily hunting for that old policeman, but I can't find the beast, which is most annoying, as I'm spoiling for my revenge.

Please admit:—-
Name:- 'Rip' Miss W.'s dog.
Destination:- E34 a
Business:- To assist in the preparation
of meals for munition workers.
Note: This pass is not transferable. Bearer
must produce the same when required and
answer all questions put by the police
or other persons in authority.

Since then I have been busily hunting
for that old policeman, but I can't find
the beast, which is most annoying as
I'm spoiling for revenge.

[handwritten annotation] *Been around Gty, 12.12.16*

There is one other dog in the Arsenal who lives with the gunners in the testing pits, but he hasn't a pass. He has a very beautiful brass-studded collar bearing this inscription: 'I am Barney, the Proof Butts Dog, but whose dog are you?'

During the air raid in April, Rip rushed out to bark at the guns and fell in the ditch that runs round the danger area. This ditch is full of picric acid and the result was first that he was very sick, and secondly, for months he was bright canary yellow, bright as a daffodil. No amount of baths would take it off. It wasn't until he changed his coat in the autumn that he became white again. He really looked most peculiar.

Wednesday, 12 April
The new job at Abbey Wood.

Feel rather appalled at the size of the morsel I have bitten off. Hope I shall be able to masticate it alright, but have my doubts. The show has grown so rapidly that the organization, equipment etc. hasn't been able to keep up with it. There aren't enough paid cooks and chars, nor enough volunteers, nor enough cups, saucers, plates, saucepans or gas ovens, or anything else.

The result is frightful chaos and disorder, and dirt. No one has time to scrub or polish, all you do is to feed the hungry swarms somehow or no how. If you can't find a spoon, you serve the pudding with a fork or a carving knife. If you can't find a plate, you put it on a saucer and give the purchaser a teaspoon to eat it with. Oh, it's the very dickens. The present head is quite nice and by no means a fool, but she cheerfully admits it has got quite beyond her and gaily says, 'Well, I wish you joy. It's the very devil.' Oh well, now I'm in for it; I've just got to make a sporting effort I suppose, or perish in the attempt.

Tuesday, 2 May
Not much hope of getting this straight. It is impossible to get the Committee to buck up and really do something serious. Meanwhile, the girls have increased from 600 to 700, and the crockery considerably reduced. The canteen continues to grow apace. We now have 700 or more to tea. I have been allowed one extra charwoman as against 100 girls, which helps a bit, but not much.

The other day, Miss B. and I went over to a canteen run by Lockhart Cubitt's girls. [Lockhart Cubitt were, and still are, a professional catering company.] They have all modern appliances, steamers, boilers, hot water supplier etc. All supplies come by van from the main stores as the superintendent has no buying to do and no tussles with tradesmen, and no complicated accounts.

For staff compare:

Lockhart: 600 girls	No: 2 700 girls
1 manager	1 manageress
3 men cooks	1 cook
2 kitchen boys	3 chars
2 charwomen	8–11 volunteers
16 waitresses	
7 counterhands	

When I enumerated our staff and lack of equipment to the manager, he simply said, impossible, couldn't be done on those lines.

We have no proper equipment, just three gas stoves, ordinary pots and pans and not enough of them, and boilers that have to be filled by hand with jugs.

For staff: Manageress, who has to do all her own ordering, making of contracts, accounts etc. also look after incompetent volunteers.

The result is that one is always in a frantic scramble. I have to bustle round, make tea, serve out dinners, stop the volunteers doing silly things, even sometimes help peel the potatoes, while my own work of catering has to go hang and just be squeezed in at odd moments. I shall stick it for the present until I have made it pay, which it doesn't at present, and then I shall strike for a really adequate staff. Probably they will squash me, and if so, I shall just go elsewhere; there is no satisfaction or credit in trying to make bricks without straw, and not even the greatest genius can make a success of the job. Not even I!!

Thursday, 4 May
Spent Easter at North Bromley in a queer little inn, very smart outside and very old inside, and had a very jolly time with Miss B. I came back to find that my landlord and lady had not returned (I do not lodge with Miss B. now), so went to bed in an empty house. At 11.00, a wild uproar of guns. I skipped out of bed and flew to the bathroom window, and there high up was a Zep looking just like a little sausage in the sky. All round her (as it seemed) shells were bursting, and three or four searchlights were playing full upon her. The ordinary shells give no light till they burst but the incendiary shells have a long, dull red tail, like a rocket, behind them. Besides these there were a few 'Star Shells', which give a brilliant light for a few moments, rather similar to that given by magnesium wire. She came on for a bit, but finding things a bit too hot for her, turned tail and bolted. After she had been in the searchlight for nearly ten minutes, I suddenly heard an awed voice in a neighbouring back garden remark, 'Oh look, there it is!' No bombs were dropped. The only damage was that all the windows in the next street, opposite one of the guns, were smashed.

Saturday, 20 May
I have given notice. I stated all my reasons. The result was an agitated letter from Miss Fry.
Why wouldn't I stay?
Did I want more money?
Was it private reasons?
Didn't I like her personally?
If they gave me more help would I stay?
To all of which I answered NO, and remained obdurate. Since then I have had three similar visits from various members of the Committee as

they can't find anyone else to take it on. I have consented to stay on until 1 July, to oblige, but not longer. Isn't it nice to be so treasured? The place is so disorganized that it would need a tremendous upheaval to get it right, not 'one more char', which is what they would relapse into as soon as they thought I had settled down. Well, I have paid off all the original cost of equipment and bought a lot of new equipment, and I have left them a balance of £150, so they ought to be thankful, though they never showed the slightest appreciation of my efforts until I gave notice. Now no amount of flattery and butter is too much for them to apply. But I shan't stay. They would only relapse into their wicked old ways.

Monday, 12 June

An awful old party has been 'helping' this week, Lady Clarke. She announced that she meant to teach the girls better manners. They must learn to say 'please' and 'thank you'. Presently, up comes a girl:

'Pennyworth of cheese.'

'What?' says Lady Clarke, 'what?' expecting her to add please.

'Huh,' says the girl, 'there's a nice way to speak to anyone. "Wot, wot." Why don't you say, "I beg your pardon, missus," if you can't hear?'

'My dear girl,' says Lady Clarke, 'where did you learn your manners?'

'Not where you learnt yours, thank the Lord.'

We haven't had much trouble with Her Ladyship since. She is singularly quiet and inoffensive.

Saturday, 22 July

Today I was shown over the factory as a great favour. First, I saw the cordite made into charges. Each charge consists of five or six little bagfuls and a core. Each little bag is shaped like a lifebelt.

The quantity of cordite it contains has to be weighed to a pin's head (hair's breadth). Even the silk it is sewn up with is weighed so as to get absolute accuracy. Each bag contains a different weight, and the five or six are then put one on top of the other and the core threaded through them.

The core is made of a bundle of cordite, like a faggot or strings of glue, and smells like it too. The whole charge is then packed into a case (box) containing the detonator.

Then I was shown the lyddite works. This is a brilliant canary yellow powder (picric acid) and comes in wooden tubs. It is then sifted. The house (windows, floor, walls) in which this is done are stained bright yellow, and so are the faces of the workers. As soon as you go in, the lyddite in the air gets into your nose and mouth and makes you sneeze and splutter as if you had violent hay fever. It gives you a horrid bitter taste at the back of your throat.

After this, the acid is put into big cans and stood in tanks, where it is boiled until it melts into a clear liquid like vinegar. It is then poured into the shell case, but a mould is inserted before it has time to solidify. This mould when drawn out leaves a space down the middle of the shell. Before it is drawn out, beeswax is passed in and then several cardboard washers put in. Then the mould is replaced by a candle-shaped exploder of TNT, or tetrol, or some other very high explosive. After this, the fuse cap is screwed in, then two screws have to be put in to hold it firm. The holes for these screws must not be drilled straight into the decorator. If they do, the thing explodes.

The fuse has a red cross marked where the detonator is, as a warning, and the girls must be careful not to drill their screw holes at this point. If they do, they go to glory. One girl did this a few weeks ago, but of course it is just sheer carelessness if they do.

After the fuse is screwed in, the shells are painted with distinctive colours. Its date and place of manufacture is stencilled on it and then they are packed in twos in a box with two charges. On the box, forty different stencils have to be put on before it is ready to be dispatched to the Germans. Only small shells are made here.

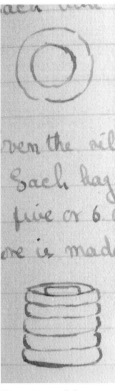

Drawings of the shells, how they are filled and where the screw holes should be.

Tuesday, 8 August
Buckie is now running two small canteens in the Arsenal for Lady Londonderry's Womens Legion. Each is for about 300. They are very nicely decorated and equipped. There is 'G [a drawn crown] R' [i.e., the royal crest] on the cups, plates and saucepans, even on the rolling pin and mincer. Also, there are to be paid workers, but unfortunately the pay isn't very good, so that I doubt whether good helpers will be obtainable at the

Women munitions workers with 6-inch howitzer shells, at the Chilwell ammunition factory, Nottinghamshire, 1917.
Wikimedia Commons

salary offered. I am to be cook in one at 25/-. Not so much as I had at Abbey Wood, but I hope it won't be such heavy, killing work.

Today we heard we had been allotted a government hut. As soon as we can collect the necessary furniture, we are going to move in. The government has built thousands of huts on every bit of spare land round here, in order to house all the Arsenal workers. The office to which we had to go to claim it is only open from 1.00–2.00 and 6.00–7.00, hours when we cannot get off. However, I managed to scramble down there one day at a few minutes past 7.00 and persuaded the man to attend to me. I happened to have heard by chance that he had been very late arriving, so when he said he was locking up and could not attend to me, I said, 'Well, you were late this morning and I am late this evening, so we are both about quits?'

Gabrielle and Rip walking up to the front door of her hut.

There are five rooms in our palace, three bedrooms, a parlour, and a back kitchen/scullery. Also, there is a tiny larder and coal cellar, and another useful little abode.

There is a gas stove and a copper in the scullery and a coal range in the parlour. A bath can be fixed for an extra 6d a week in rent, which then makes it come to 10/- a week. We also have quite a large garden. Outside, the huts look quite palatial, being made of tarred wood with little lattice porches to the back doors. The front doors are plain and unadorned. I don't know why the back is so beautiful. Please observe the government dustbin at the back door. It is nearly as large as the house.

Tuesday, 15 August
We have quite settled down in the hut. When we first moved in we only had a bed, a chair each and a big packing case for a table. Now we are most luxurious – deckchairs and a table, washstands, even saucepans and a flat iron. One of the neighbours comes in twice a week to clean it up.

The canteens are running well and paying well, but as I feared, it is difficult to get and keep good workers at 15/-. The work is hard and the hours very long – twelve hours a day. They find that in the sheds they can earn 25/- to £3, or even more, for the same number of hours and not at such high pressure, so naturally, as soon as they get a chance they leave the canteen and go to work in the sheds. This makes it very hard for the heads as we are perpetually shorthanded.

Tuesday, 12 September

Miss Buckpitt is leaving here and going to start a big men's canteen at the other side of the Arsenal. She doesn't want to move at all, but the Committee have persuaded her into it. It is too much to have to start one place after another like this, as at first the staff is often short and things in a muddle. We often have to work fourteen hours or more to put things through.

Things here are just beginning to settle down and go smoothly, and if she starts a new one it will mean all the slavery all over again. It doesn't hurt me to slave fourteen hours or more a day and to miss one's day off three or four times in succession for a time, but it isn't the sort of thing one wants to be at perpetually. However, they have told her it's her duty, that they can't find anyone else to do it, and if she will only do it this once, she won't be uprooted any more, so she has consented.

The second small canteen is to be run independently and I am to be supervisor of this one. Of course, this is a step up; 35/- instead of 25/-, and a further rise to 40/- in a month's time. But it will be deadly dull. There will be no one to speak to except the kitchen hands and the waitresses, and I'm not looking forward to it at all.

Tuesday, 19 September

Miss B. has just been checking the equipment for her new canteen, F14. It is to cater for 800 men. As usual, it seems to have been selected by a lunatic. There are no cups and saucers, but 1,400 small teapots, big enough for one person. Just imagine in a canteen giving each person a separate pot of tea. But that's just like the Office of Works. They never seem to follow any plan in equipping a place.

Some of their other little jokes are as follows:

The National Canteen, Abbeywood, had a huge sausage machine, which it took three charwomen to turn. This was in place of a mincer. They had five carving knives but no forks. There was a tiny little steel 4 inches long (for sharpening said knives).

E105, for the use of the kitchen workers, there were thirty-six roller towels and thirty-six rollers to hang them on. Evidently, they imagined that all the towels have to be hung up at once. There were only eight workers in the kitchen. There were 100 vinegar cruets and fourteen huge frying pans. Even to poach an egg you had to use a frying pan 15 inches across.

E34, intended for 300 girls, has thirty-six huge brown dustsheets, no one knows what for, three meat covers so small that they wouldn't even cover a leg of mutton successfully. We have only thirty-six tumblers, but 350 teapots. No scales. When one was requisitioned, one with a flat slab instead of a scoop was sent, off which flour etc. always falls. There are only two brooms but five dozen dusters.

D49, also for 300 girls, has no dust sheets but they have 300 tumblers as against our thirty-six. They have eighty-four brooms as against our two! They had no weighing scales either, and when they requisitioned one they got a large platform weighing engine, which stands on the ground, for whole flour sacks or luggage. On this they are expected, I suppose, to weigh 1oz of baking powder or 1d worth of cheese. There must be great minds at work in the Office of Works.

Sunday, 1 October
Am getting rather fed up. Last week, two of my women didn't turn up. On Wed, the cashier was taken suddenly ill. The Committee undertook to send new workers. On the following Monday, two very beautiful ladies arrived from the London Office and informed me I was to employ them at £1 a week. Of course, I didn't want two such duchesses; what I wanted was one cashier and three washers up. However, I shifted the staff around a bit and put one in as cashier and the other as night head. In about a week, all sorts of rumours and scandals were afloat, and one morning I found the following chalked on the door:

Smoking Concerts Held Here Every Night
All Gentlemen Cordially invited
But Be Sure
&
Leave Your Wives Behind.

So the two lovely ladies had to be hustled off in double-quick time. Apparently, no enquiries had been made and no references taken up when they were engaged by the Hon. Sec in London.

The result was I was left two short, and as it was the fault of the Committee for sending such creatures, I asked them to find me new ones. No one came for over a week, then a very pretty, feeble little person of sixteen, who of course is going to be more trouble than she is worth.

Thursday, 5 October

When Miss B. told Lady Londonderry she would not wear the Women's Legion uniform, a khaki get-up, as she was already wearing her own Cheltenham uniform, Lady L. replied that she thought that would do. Now that Miss B. has done all their dirty work and started four new canteens, Lady L. suddenly announces that she must wear the khaki Women's Legion uniform. Miss B. has refused.

Sunday, 8 October

Miss B. has resigned on account of this fuss over the uniform. I think she is quite right under the circumstances; they should have insisted at first if they meant to, not let her do all the dirty work for them first. I also wear the Cheltenham Dame's uniform, so when the Hon. Sec came down to E34 today, I said that of course, what applied to Miss B. applied to me. 'Oh,' said Mr Longstaff, 'You aren't going to resign too are you? Oh Damn!'

He is much put out as my and Miss B.'s canteen (E34 and F14) are the only ones that never give any trouble, as he told us the other day. But I am glad to be leaving. We couldn't have gone on as we have been doing for ever. Owing to the muddles of the London Committee, we were always shorthanded, the staff was always grousing about the wages, and ever since I have come to Woolwich, I have done twelve or thirteen or even fourteen hours a day full speed ahead, with hardly time to bolt my meals, often for weeks at a time. I've had no day off on four or five occasions. I've done a night shift in between two day shifts, which means thirty-six hours' continuous work. You can't go on with that sort of thing for ever. Also, if Miss B. leaves the neighbourhood, I shall have to leave the hut and I can't very well go back to rooms as there aren't any to be got.

Saturday, 14 October

No end of Zep excitements lately. A few weeks ago, we heard distant guns in the middle of the night, and then some hours later, more guns, still a long way off. We waited a few minutes and then went into the road. There was a funny whirring noise, which we took to be the motors that carry round the anti-aircraft guns. There was no firing and no searchlights. Then suddenly up came the searchlights and there was the Zep, so low you could see the cars hanging underneath and almost over our heads, it seemed. We just turned and scooted. There was a tremendous din of firing, and then we heard a number of big bangs and a great smell of smoke, and things began to patter on the roof. My word, were we scared. We stood in the kitchen not daring to breathe and heard the whirring noise go right over our heads. When we ventured out to look, the beast was making off towards the Thames, having passed right over the hutments. I thought I really was dead that time.

The next morning, on our way to work, we passed three villas completely wrecked, and every window all down the street was smashed. Seven people were killed. These houses were only about 200 yards from the hut, so no wonder we were scared. A lot more damage was done and several more killed at Greenwich and other places. No one knows exactly why, but certainly there was something wrong for the searchlights to let her get so low before lighting up and giving the guns a chance. Some say a German spy put the leading searchlight out of action (i.e. the one the others have to follow), others, that the officers in charge all went to a dance, and others that the men who work the searchlights got drunk. You can believe what you like, but certainly something was wrong somewhere.

After this scare we got four days' holiday in place of the many postponed bank holidays. We went to Deal and had a jolly time. It is a dear old place. The beach is full of trenches, barbed wire and dugouts. When it rained we went and sat in one. Out at sea is a little fleet of destroyers who search each boat that goes up or down the Channel. You see the destroyers in the middle and a little row of steamers on each side meekly waiting to be searched.

We came home on Sunday night ready to start work on Monday, and had a fearful struggle to get home, loaded with a dog and various packages. We hadn't been long in bed when we again heard guns. We went out and saw a Zep far away to the south. I used to think a Zep raid rather exciting but since the last, I feel I've had quite enough. Instead of feeling pleasantly thrilled, I just feel squirmy inside and very cold and clammy. However, it disappeared and the firing ceased.

In about two hours it began again, so again we trotted out but could see nothing. All this time we had been sitting in the cottage drinking tea and discussing the war with our neighbour's family and our neighbour's neighbour's family. We were just going back to our own hut when we heard wild cheering and saw the whole sky turn red, and then we saw the Zep in flames to the north. She just came floating gently down until a big piece of burning stuff fell off, and then she nosedived to the earth and it was all dark again except for two little red lights twirling madly about where she fell.

I never heard such a noise in my life. All the hooters in the Arsenal and on the barges yelled at once, and all the workers in the Arsenal roared and shrieked. All the boys in the YMCA hostel up the road sang *Tipperary* and all the neighbours scuttled about congratulating each other. Even staid, respectable Buckie and I danced around each other and crowed.

Later, we heard that the twirling red lights were Robinson and another airman doing a sort of war dance of loops and spirals over their enemy's remains. This was the Cuffley Zep. A few days later, we saw the second one come down at Potters Bar, and not long after that, the third. Of course, there were others brought down, but not in flames, and so of course they were not visible from a distance.

Although all these were some distance from Woolwich (the first one being in fact on the other side of London), they appeared quite close, say about 10 or 12 miles away. We had half a mind to start off to see it, only we had to be up so early the next morning. I'm jolly glad we didn't, for we certainly would never have got there.

Another night I was woken up by much shouting and thumping, and noise of broken glass. In the morning the amiable little boy from next door shouted to me across the garden palings: 'Say, did you hear the row last night? That was the copper from across the road, thought we'd got his wife in our back kitchen – and we had, too! He's broke all the winders in the front.' What it is to be an East Ender!!

What they had seen was Lieutenant William Leefe Robinson shooting down the Schutte-Lanz SL 11, a small Zeppelin . He was awarded the Victoria Cross for his feat.

A watercolour of London, with Westminster Bridge on the right-hand side, by Joan Mary, showing the view from her flat window. The painting is now in the Stroud Museum.

Thursday, 2 November

Have escaped from Woolwich at last! The dirt and the noise and dirty swearing people were beginning to get on my nerves a bit.

We had in a furniture dealer, and as we imagined, got rid of practically all our belongings. But when it really came to the point, we had the following packages:

2 trunks	1 despatch case
1 hat box	1 dressing case
1 gladstone	1 dog
1 folding bed	1 tin box
4 chairs	1 handle umbrella
1 mattress	2 bicycles
1 dog basket	
1 handbag	

The carriers of both bikes were packed with things that could not be stuffed in anywhere else. Never mind, we've escaped, that's what matters.

Buckie has got rooms in London and I am staying at Joan's [sister] flat, and we are both looking for work.

We have interviewed one artistic diaphanous lady with a view to becoming housemaid and cook respectively. She offered £40 and £30 per annum, and all she wanted was to have good cooking and no trouble; didn't mention whether she would care to have the house kept clean or not, probably not. We didn't sign on.

Next, I saw an advert for girls to drive Lyons' bread carts (horse-drawn) and sell their bread and cakes, so I went down to Cadby Hall and was interviewed by a fat porpoise of a man (Mr Glucksteen) and two skinny little men who sat in a row and goggled at me. The interview was some thing like this:

'Can you drive.'

'Yes.'

'Do you know London?'

'Not much.'

'What is the cost of five loaves at 3/4d?'

Dead Silence.

Your wartime car-woman, 1915–19. This picture was submitted to Lyons Mail *in 1969 by a Mrs Gittins, who was the manager of a J. Lyons' shop in Paddington during the First World War.*
London Metropolitan Archive

'Well then, what is the cost of four loaves at 5 and 3/4d?'

Deader silence.

I was not found suitable but was asked if I would like to be a seater in the restaurant at a salary of £1 a week. Didn't know what a seater was so I stuck my nose in the air and said £1 wasn't enough. He said there were plenty of chances of advancement. I still sniffed. Then he asked what money I had been taking, and I said 35/- and my board, and made, or tried to make, a dignified exit.

I've asked ever so many people who think they are good at arithmetic the price of four loaves at 5 and 3/4d and no one seems to be able to do it without at least ten minutes' deep thought, so I'm not such a hopeless fool after all.

J. Lyons: horse-drawn bread sales vans during WWI

J. Lyons began as a joint enterprise between Joseph Lyons and his brothers-in-law, the Glucksteins. It was a Mr Gluckstein who interviewed Bobby.

J. Lyons began selling bread in 1894. The door-to-door sale of bread from handcarts was so successful that horse-drawn vans were soon employed. By 1900, there were five horse-drawn vans. By 1920, each morning, 200 horse-drawn vans of various types left Cadby Hall from the extensive stables there, to deliver bread all over West London.

Numbered at more than a hundred at the start of the war, the bakery roundsmen didn't hesitate to volunteer for the services. With some trepidation on the part of the directors, their jobs were taken over by women. The women kept the bakery rounds not only functioning, but secure for the men returning after the war. Their success can be judged by the fact that there were 140 rounds by 1922, and the service continued to grow.

(Peter Bird, *The First Food Empire*, Phillimore, 2000)

It is the funniest thing in the world being an out of worker.

After this, we rubbed at several other jobs such as another canteen at Darlington, housekeeper and cook at Bristol Infirmary, the same at a girl's school in Studley, and so on.

Then we heard that Women Police were badly needed so went to their offices to see what that was like. All the Women Police we saw were very smart in a very dapper uniform of navy blue. We were interviewed by an inspector who was very nice, and discovered the following details:

They are anxious to get Women Police recognized as an official branch of the men's police to specially deal with women and children. So far, they haven't had recognition for their work, only a sort of 'toleration', but certain county and borough councils have employed WPs on their own responsibility, paying them out of local rates and taxes. They work independently of the men police and are not sworn in.

Also, a few county police associations have done the same, and in a few cases they have actually sworn them in like the men.

But the Government (i.e Ministry of Munitions) have recognized them and employed them largely inside factories to control the women workers (i.e. munitions workers), and this is what they want recruits for. Pay is £2 a week, which isn't bad, but recruits have to buy their own uniform. They have taken up our references and if we are accepted, I think we shall go alright; it sounds nice.

A cutting that Bobby kept from Home Chat *magazine of 3 March 1917. The original caption reads: 'In answer to an advertisement for Women Police for Munition Works – to guard against the carelessness of workers – hundreds of applications came in. Here are a few of the applicants. By the by, a specially interesting article will appear in* Home Chat *next week, entitled "Why So Many Girls Broke Down".'*

Sunday, 3 December
Have been at home nearly ten days and have now been summoned by the Women Police to begin training, so am back again in Joan's flat to go to the office tomorrow for my final lecture on the duties of a WP.

WOMEN POLICE

Women police officers first came into being during the First World War. There was a great deal of politics and two organizations involved. The Women's Police Volunteers(WPV), who became the Women's Police Service (WPS), were expected to be 'educated gentlewomen', were rather more radical and had links with the suffragette movement. The National Union of Working Women (NUWW) deplored militant feminists and saw themselves more as aides to the male police than moral guardians.

At the end of the war, when the request was made that the WPS should be incorporated into a women's police force, the comment was made that they were 'too educated' and would 'irritate' the male officers. As a result, the post-war women's police service was recruited from the NUWW.

The concerns in 1914 seem to have been largely about the moral behaviour of women, who from the start of the war had much greater social freedom. Bobby, in 1979, remarks on the irrelevance of her training: 'It was all talk about sex troubles and so on. Nothing to do with what we did.'

During the First World War very few of the women police were 'sworn' and therefore were denied the power of arrest. Bobby writes of the problem this caused in the factories, and in the 1979 interviews, when asked further about it, she says, with a smile in her voice, 'Well, we had a hard hat.'

None of the politics is relevant here. It never interested our diarist. What was relevant to her was that the WPV in 1915 signed a contract with the Ministry of Munitions to supply uniformed women police as lady supervisors in munitions factories. Whereas most of the WPVs were unpaid, those in the munitions factories were paid a weekly wage.

From 1914 to 1920, about 1,000 women were trained as police officers and 90 per cent of them were employed in munitions factories.

Monday, 4 December

There are about twenty other recruits; some have been here for about a week, others, like ourselves, have just begun. Most are ladies, a much better class, in fact, quite a different class to a policeman.

We had a lecture, and drill; tomorrow we go to a police court.

Gabrielle and her police constable colleagues when training. She is second from the left on the back row.

Thursday, 14 December

Training lasts a fortnight and consists of lectures, attending police courts and children's courts and taking notes, drill, patrolling in the evenings and a little general work. The patrolling is with a woman police sergeant at night, especially around Victoria Station and other rather lively neighbourhoods.

For general training we are usually sent down to Paddington, where two women police are employed by the District Council. We watched them at work. They help children across the roads when coming to and from school, patrol the streets, see children aren't taken inside pubs, report broken area steps or railings etc. to the sanitary inspector. The permanent women police act occasionally as probation officers at the request of the court.

But we haven't been near a factory or heard anything about factories, which seems odd as we are being trained for factory work. Buckie and I are destined for a factory at Chester.

Wednesday, 20 December

Here we are in Chester. Very nice rooms, very nice landlady, very nice place and very nice work.

There are three shifts: 5.30 am to 2.00 pm, 2.00 pm to 11.00 pm and 10.00 pm to 6.00 am. We do afternoon and morning alternately, with an occasional night, but night work doesn't come very often as only two people do that at a time, whereas there are eight or nine by day. The factory is about 5 miles from Chester and you go by train. On the morning shift you have to rise at 4.00 am. Horrid! Still, you get the afternoon to yourself, and as the work is not too hard you aren't too exhausted to enjoy yourself, as at Woolwich.

The work consists of the following duties:

Searching incoming workers for matches, cigarettes spirits etc. in pockets, baskets etc.
Searching outgoing workers for stolen property.
Keeping guard at the gate and allowing no one to enter without a pass.
Conducting stray visitors round and dealing with new workers, lost passes, lost clock cards etc.
Keeping order in the clocking shed. Locking and unlocking it.

Keeping the office where clerks etc. sign on and off, enquiries
    are made, visitors passes visa'd and entered etc.
Patrolling to see that no one is larking or slacking.

We take turns at all these various jobs, none of which were taught us
during training. We have two hours off for meals, so life is not too
strenuous.

Chester is a lovely old town of half-timbered houses, a fine cathedral,
a very interesting old church and also a complete city wall you can walk
all the way round, about 3 miles. The river is good for boating, so in the
summer I shall try and learn how to row properly. Do you remember how
Joan and I used to splash round at Tewksbury and Evesham, and how you
scandalized the neighbourhood by paddling a canoe *a la* the university
with its head in the air?

Michael paddling a canoe.

A poster issued by the Ministry of Munitions of War in 1917.
Library of Congress

1917

Friday, 5 January

Marching orders again! This time, instead of giving or getting notice, we have been promoted. Buckie to sub-inspector and me to sergeant. We both go to Pembrey in South Wales in three days' time.

But I must say a little more about this place. The factory is occupied making the following:

Sulphuric acid	Nitric acid	
Oleum	Guncotton	TNT

The result is the most terrific collection of stinks, or 'fumes', to put it less baldly, that you could possibly imagine. For patrolling purposes it is divided into four areas:

1. The Grills, consisting of five sulphur burners, acid coolers, platinizing plant etc. The burners each have forty furnaces, twenty doors on either side. Occasionally for cleaning purposes, 'the blowers are taken off.' Exactly what that means, I don't know, but the result is most fascinating.

Out of each furnace door and each damper comes a huge sky-blue flame 3 or 4 feet long so that the whole place is an avenue of gorgeous colour. Then first one and then another flame begins to get pink at the base and then pink all over, then they begin to have flame-coloured tips and lemon-yellow bases, and then they gradually turn yellow to pink to green, and from green to deep, rich blue. After that they begin to flicker out, but while it lasts it is the most wonderful display of colour you could possibly see. Devonshire Park fireworks are [a] mere glimmer to it.

When the blowers are on, the Grills hasn't much to recommend it, being enriched with an evil sulphurous smell such as I always imagined was reserved for the Devil and his angels exclusively. I wonder if they ever take the blowers off down there!

2. Guncotton. The first few times you go round you think, 'What an interesting place', and are just brimming over with questions. Then one joyous day you are taken round by the sergeant and told exactly what everything is for and how everything is done. The next time or two, you are quite happy trotting round new constables and airing all your recently acquired knowledge. After a bit, they know as much as you do, or they think they do. After that, the guncotton ceases to interest you and the evil smell from the guncotton retorts becomes more noticeable.

3. The TNT stinks; no other word describes it – an evil, sickly chokey smell that makes you cough until you feel sick. But even the TNT is not so absolutely suffocating and overwhelming as the:

4. Middle Section. Here sulphuric is turned into nitric, and nitric into oleum. The air is filled with white fumes and yellow fumes and brown fumes. The particles of acid land on your face and make you nearly mad with a feeling like pins and needles, only more so, and they land on your clothes and make brown spots all over them, and they rot your hankies so that they come back from the laundry in rags, and they get up your nose and down your throat and into your eyes so that you are blind and speechless by the time you escape.

All over the place, there are, to cheer you on your way, notices telling you what to do if anyone swallows brown fumes:

If concerned, give an emetic.

If blue in the face, apply artificial respiration, and if necessary, oxygen.

Being quite sure you have swallowed numberless brown fumes, this is distinctly cheering. Each time you leave Middle Section, you feel like Dante returning from Hell.

Sunday, 14 January

Pembrey is the back of beyond. It's a little coal mining village with a minute harbour, and the remains of what was once a silver works, and thereby hangs a tale. This silver works belonged to Joe and Austen Chamberlain and Family. [Austen was Joe's son from his first marriage; Joe's younger son (and Austen's half-brother) was British Prime Minister Neville Chamberlain.] The directors, managers, foremen, and even the workmen waxed exceedingly fat on the said silver works. If anyone wished to build a house, they went to the works with a horse and cart and fetched the necessary bricks, wood tiles etc. If anyone needed coal, they did likewise. In fact, they say that every house in Pembrey was built out of these works. The only people who didn't do well out of it were Joe and family. At length, Austen came down to hold an enquiry into the matter and found so many things that needed enquiring into that he found it quicker and cheaper to close down the works, and they have remained closed ever since – an illustration of that wise little rhyme:

Taffy was a Welshman
Taffy was a thief.

The factory is 3½ miles from Pembrey. The town mostly consists of rather dismal-looking cement houses, some larger, some smaller, but most fairly pretentious. They have gas laid on everywhere and smart little tiled paths leading up to the doors, but no water and no drains. Very Welsh.

So far, we are living in Swansea, 20 miles away and an hour's journey by 'Shift train', but if we can succeed in getting rooms nearer we shall move. But rooms are by no means easy to get.

We now have got very nice clean rooms in Pembrey, only the landlady dislikes doing any cooking and gives us nothing but slack on the fires.

The factory is built on the Burrows (i.e. sand hills), the most desolate spot in this world. The factory sheds are built in amongst these sand hills; in fact, where the most dangerous work is done, the sheds are actually inside the hills. The hill is scooped out in the middle and an entrance into the crater thus formed by means of a tunnel, and thus the shed is built with a large mound of sand all round it and is entered by this small tunnel through the mound. In this way, the sheds are quite invisible from outside.

This part of the factory doesn't look like a factory at all, more like a gigantic rabbit warren than anything else. In these very dangerous sheds only five or six workers are allowed in at a time, and if an extra person wants to go in, one of those inside must come out. These are the 'sieving sheds', where the powder intended for making cordite and ballistite is put through a metal sieve.

This factory makes TNT, guncotton, cordite and ballistite.

Guncotton is made in the following way. The cotton is first put through the teasing machine, and then it is picked over by hand and sent to the acid room, where it is soaked in a mixture of nitric [acid], sulphuric [acid], oleum [a solution of sulphur trioxide in sulphuric acid] and water in big earthenware ewers. Then it is taken out and sent to the vat house, where it is boiled in soda and water. From here it goes to the pulping house. At this stage it looks a bit like very draggled bits of cotton wool floating in a brownish liquid. In the pulping house it is stirred round and run between rollers till it becomes a smooth cream-coloured mass, like rather thin porridge. From the pulping house it passes on to the press house, where it is pressed into blocks that resemble yellow soap, only it is more buff than yellow. Some of this is used as it is for laying mines etc., but a good deal is ground down into powder and made into cordite.

To make it into cordite a certain amount of nitroglycerine is mixed with it. It is then called paste, though it isn't the least like paste. It is a dry but slightly greasy powder, very like flour into which a certain amount of fat has been rubbed in order to make a cake. This paste is then sent to incorporating mills, where it is mixed with ether and alcohol and minimal jelly into a dough, and sent on to the press houses. Here the dough is put into cylinders, hydraulic pressure is applied and it passes out into long tubes like macaroni, only brown, and the hole up the centre much smaller, hardly visible, in fact.

The tubes are sent to the stoves, which are like immense linen cupboards with shelves all round. There they are kept at about the same heat as a linen cupboard for several days. From being tough but pliable like string, they become hard, semi-transparent and very wiry, like whalebone. Thence they are sent to the blending house. In the blending house, defective and broken pieces are detected and thrown out by banging bunches of the cordite against the table edges, and the different trays full of cordite are mixed together to ensure uniformity of strength. That is to say, a girl takes two or three pieces from each of a dozen trays and puts them into a box, which is screwed down when full, labelled and sealed, and is then ready to be despatched to the filling factory.

The danger buildings at Pembrey.

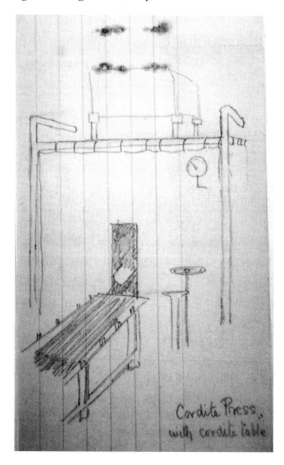

Cordite Press,
with cordite table

The cordite press with cordite table.

135

FEMALE MUNITION WORKERS

More than 900,000 women of all ages worked in munitions factories during the First World War. Though they were paid far less than the men, it was nevertheless good money for women workers. The work, however, as will emerge from the diaries, was both unhealthy and dangerous. About 400 women were killed in TNT factory accidents during the war.

Women produced 80 per cent of the weapons and shells used by the Army.

Bobby cut these pictures from a publication called Women Workers during The Big War. *They show cotton pulping, guncotton boiling and cordite pressing.*

Guncotton pulping.

Guncotton boiling.

Cordite pressing.

Saturday, 10 March

The girls here are very rough, so are the conditions. Their language is sometimes too terrible. But they are also very impressionable, shrieking with rage one minute and on quite friendly terms the next.

The previous sub-inspector had only one sergeant and three constables under her, and they managed to get themselves heartily detested by the workers, with the result that for a policewoman to so much as show herself was a signal for all the girls to shriek and boo. They several times threatened to duck the sub-inspector and did once throw a basin of dirty water over her.

One of our duties here is to get the girls out of their dining room and back to work at the proper time. When Buckie and the three constables first attempted this in real earnest they first hooted and booed, and then assembled outside and announced they would down the first policewoman who came near them. However, Buckie and I marched boldly in among them and held forth. By and by, one or two cried out to the booers to 'shut up' as we'd got a bit of pluck anyhow, but it took one and a half hours of argument and entreaty to get them back. But they haven't been so troublesome ever since.

The ether in the cordite affects the girls. It gives some headaches, hysteria, and sometimes fits. If a worker has the least tendency to epilepsy, even if she has never shown it before, the ether will bring it out. There are fifteen or twenty girls who get these fits. On a heavy, windless night we sometimes have thirty girls overcome by the fumes in one way or another. Girls who show any signs of epilepsy ought really to be discharged or found other work, as if they stay on in the cordite sheds, they may become confirmed epileptics and have fits even when not exposed to the fumes. However, this is not done. Some of the girls have twelve fits, one after another.

When these girls get taken ill, we are generally called in to render what assistance we can and take the sick girls up to the surgery on a stretcher. There are only three beds there, and so if these are full we do the best we can to make them comfortable in the dining rooms. In this way we have begun to win their confidence, and some who were most aggressive at first are beginning to be friendly.

I find these girls here much more interesting than those at Chester. [The munitions factory was at Queensferry, just a few miles away from Chester.] They are so full of life and cheerful and there are so many 'characters' amongst them, and a great many different types. Of course, there is a huge number: 800 in one section and about 500 in other sections in each shift, making a total of 3,900 women workers. Some of these are girls from lonely little sheep farms in the mountains; these speak only Welsh or a very little broken English, and are very good sorts, though rough.

Then there are the wives and other relatives of the miners, from the Rhondda Valley and other coal pits near. They are very full of socialistic theories and are perpetually getting up strikes in true Tonypandy style. [Bobby is referring to the Tonypandy, or Rhondda, riots of 1910 and 1911, when mine workers protested about regulations to prices and wages set by a cartel of mining companies in South Wales.] But although so violent when thy think they are being trampled on, they are very easily influenced by a little oratory and as soon as they have made up their minds 'to go back', they become as meek as lambs, if you spout at them long enough.

A number of girls are from the Swansea Docks, and some of these are really bad characters. They are a mixed lot, a different type from the other Welsh girls. Some are descended from a colony of Germans who settled in the Gower Peninsula many years ago, with of course a large admixture of other races – Welsh, English, Irish, and many foreign nations, with more than a touch of the tar brush sometimes.

There is one girl here, half Negress, who is the most extraordinary mimic. She keeps the other girls in fits while she imitates the matrons, foremen, chemist, Women Police etc. She also gets up concerts during the meal times, beating time with her spoon. She has a very fine voice, as have many of the girls, so the concerts are worth listening to.

There is another girl called by all her 'pals' by the name of 'Lovey' because that is the name she gives to everyone else. She is a very jolly girl, always smiling and with a great admiration for the Women Police. We had one constable who was rather an attractive person, fascinating, with pink cheeks and grey hair and blue eyes. Lovey remarked to me one day, 'You know, Sergeant Lovey, I shall just have to kiss that little policewoman next time she searches me.' Presently in came the little policewoman very flustered, 'One of those dreadful girls has just given me a kiss, in the search room, with all the other girls watching!!'

There was a trio of very rough lots on my shift. One of these, and the worst, being a very dark, rather handsome woman of the gypsy type. These three were always in trouble, always last to go to work and too early in leaving it, and several times reported for swearing at the Women Police and so on. The dark woman too I suspected of drinking, though she was never actually drunk. At last, one day when the girls were just leaving, she bounced up to me and began to make a fearful fuss about a blouse she had taken from her in the morning because it had metal fasteners on it. She used the most fearful language and threatened to knock me down. I guessed she was more or less drunk with the ether so I took it very mildly and didn't report her.

A day or two after, she came to me and said she was very sorry. She had been told by her pal that she had been very rude and said something awful, and that she hadn't meant it. The ether had got to her head. Was I going to report her?

I said I hadn't done so.

Ever since, she has been a perfect lamb, never rude, never late, never coming down from work too early, never wearing anything she shouldn't – pins or steel hooks – in fact, a model, and she makes her two friends behave also.

I've never seen anyone change so suddenly, as it was such a very small matter to change her so completely. I suppose she thought I was sure to report her and that she was in for serious trouble, probably even dismissal, and that it took the wind out of her sails to find that nothing was going to happen at all.

There is one girl here, Mary Morgan, who gets the most appalling fits. She goes dead and stupid for a minute and then very red in the face, and then starts the most violent struggles, pulling at her own hair, scratching her own face and twisting herself into the most fearful contortions. It takes four or five of us to hold her down and prevent her from harming herself. The favourite 'cures' among the girls is to souse the sufferer with cold water, thump and slap her, shake her, pour hot tea between her teeth (although being unconscious she can't swallow), stand her on her head (when she is purple in the face already) and last but not least, sit on her 'stummick'. This particular girl told me after her last fit that she was so glad the policewomen had looked after her and kept the other girls away as last time she was that bruised in her inside that it made her sick for a week!

Tuesday, 3 April
Such a day! I was on morning shift this week so came back at three o'clock to my rooms. We are now living in Pembrey, the village being about 2½ miles from the factory. At about six o'clock there was a tremendous explosion and then a whole succession of little bangs. I rushed upstairs and from the window saw flames and smoke rising in volumes. The landlady wept and wailed and said we should all be killed, and that poor Miss Buckpitt was certainly already dead and the poor Women Police and all the girls blown to atoms.

I flew into my uniform with the old girl clinging round my neck and bolted off to the bicycle shop. There I hired a bike (my own, of course, was punctured, just when I wanted it). When I got near the factory I met several girls running for their lives. One of them stopped me to say she had left her case containing her food in the dining room, would I please be sure to go and rescue it as soon as I arrived at the factory!

When I did arrive I found the Danger Gates barred and all the girls huddled just inside them. A large shed behind the guncotton section was in flames and going off in small explosions every now and then. All the policewomen on duty were busy pacifying the girls and attending to various cases of fainting and fits. After about half an hour of this performance, the fire was put out and we were told to get the girls back to their sheds. This was easier said than done. However, after another half an hour of persuasion, one girl announced she was going back and she hoped if she perished the policewomen would remember that she had left all her money to her mother; we should find the will under the drawing room carpet. Of course, when one started, all the rest followed, and back they all marched singing:

> *What's the use of worrying?*
> *It never was worthwhile, so*
> *Pack up your troubles in your old kit bag,*
> *And smile, smile, smile.*

Tuesday, 10 April

The girls here, and the men for that matter, are very troublesome about bringing matches and cigarettes. A week or two ago, one of the Women Police actually caught a girl smoking just outside a danger building. Last week, a girl just going off duty came to the Police Office and asked me to please rescue her coat from one of the danger buildings, as she hadn't time to go back for it and catch her train. She told me I could recognize the coat because her pay slip was in the pocket. When I went for it I found the pockets full of cigarettes! Of course, the poor wretch had to be prosecuted, though it was obviously an oversight or she would not have sent me for the coat.

This factory is very badly equipped as regards the welfare of the girls. The changing rooms are fearfully crowded, long troughs are provided instead of wash basins and there is always a scarcity of soap and towels. The girls' danger clothes are often horribly dirty and in rags, and many of the outdoor workers, who should have top boots, oilskins and sou'westers, haven't them.

Although the fumes often mean sixteen or eighteen casualties a night, there are only four beds in the surgery for men and women, and they are all in the same room. There is another large surgery but it is so far from the girls' section of the factory that unless it is a serious case, girls are not taken there.

There are no drains owing to the ground being below sea level, but there could be some sort of incinerator, but there isn't. The result is a horrid, smelly swamp. There were until recently no lights in the lavatories and as these same lavatories are generally full of rats and often very dirty, the girls are afraid to go in. But by dint of great importunity, Buckie has at last persuaded the manager to put in lights. But it is really not his fault. The Lady Welfare Superintendant should see to all this, but doesn't, and what few reforms have been made have been brought about by the Women Police. This has made us very popular. In fact, the girls really do seem to almost adore us. Every time we go into the dining room to call them out to work we are presented with sweets, oranges, cakes, flowers and all kinds of offerings. Of course, we sometimes have differences of opinion, but they soon blow over.

The country round is lovely. The shore consists of most lovely firm yellow sands and we have a glorious view of Carmarthen Bay and the Mumbles from Burry Port (Pembrey) Harbour. A few weeks ago I cycled to Kidwelly. There is a very fine old castle. We also went one Saturday to Carmarthen, a very quaint, picturesque old town built on a very steep slope. They use donkeys with panniers there, like they do at Chalford.

In the market they sell lovely lustre jugs, teapots etc. and hand-painted Welsh china. There are also a number of old women in Welsh costume selling cockles. They wear funny little black bonnets and carry the tubs of cockles on their heads. You can often see these old people on the sands with their donkeys, digging cockles. The great place for cockling is Ferry Side, the dearest, sleepiest little seaside resort on the bay between Pembrey and Kidwelly.

Some day I want to take Mother and Father there. Mother would love cockling and going to Carmarthen market and Father could see Larne Castle and Kidwelly, and the sights around. But there is very little to be seen inland. The mountains come down to within a mile of the shore and the roads over are very few and very bad, and only lead to dirty little coal mining villages.

Swansea is the most repulsive spot. Huge and slummy. There is not a single decent street of shops. Even the main street is full of pokey little fried fish shops and such like. The night we arrived there first, we tried in vain to get a really good meal, being desperately hungry. The best we could do was sausages and mash, rice pudding and coffee essence.

At Pembrey, the women make money in winter by making balls of clay and slack coal for sale as fuel. The coal they collect at the pit mouths, and the clay at the sides of the harbour when the tide is out. It is most picturesque to see them coming up from the harbour in their red and black shawls with the buckets of clay on their heads.

Sergeant Guthrie is making this place uninhabitable. She is a most peculiar person: hair close-cropped like a man, thickset figure with no waist like a man, large feet like a man, and a sort of tenor voice like a man. The first two days, the girls wouldn't be searched by her; they said she was a man detective, not a policewoman at all, and there was a great fuss. Anyhow, she is a great trial and very unbalanced. When she first came we were all rather inclined to sit at her feet as we had heard she was a splendid sergeant and she had been in the Women's Police for several years.

Her first week she was on night duty, in the morning she took me aside and read me a long lecture because I had left her only two lamps, saying that at Gretna it was always the morning sergeant's duty to see to the lamps and I must please do so here. This being the first time, she would not speak to the inspector about it, but in future I must be more careful etc.

I told her if she would not speak to the inspector, I would, as I have been in the factory four months and didn't intend being called over the coals by a sergeant who hadn't been here four days, and a lot more to the same tune. The impudence of the woman – and besides, there ARE only two lamps, as she would have known if she had held her tongue and used her eyes.

Ever since, she has done all she can to dig pins into me. She searches the report, looking to find errors of spelling or badly expressed sentences. She comes early on duty in the hopes of finding my constables napping. She stays about late when my shift follows hers in case any of my constables turn up late. If she does find the least little thing wrong, she carries it straight to the inspector, instead of dropping me a hint, as I would to her if I really felt something needed putting right.

The third sergeant is the driest, dourest old Scotch woman I have ever met, and long and thin and angular withal, but not at all a bad old sort. Guthrie comes into the office and strokes this woman's hand, and kisses the top of her head and calls her darling, to Martindale's most intense indignation, who told her the other day, if she did it again she would slap her. Guthrie also started the hand-stroking and kissing game on poor Buckie, to her intense alarm and disgust. I think there must be one or two screws loose. Anyhow, she is playing off the three shifts of constables against each other, getting them to sneak on each other and their sergeants so that from being a perfectly peaceful and united squad, things have become a three-cornered battlefield and everyone is more or less miserable and full of grousings.

Sunday, 29 April

The chiefs have been down. They have offered Buckie to go and start Women Police in the new dockyards to be started at Avonmouth, leaving Guthrie here as inspector. Or for Guthrie to go to Avonmouth and B. to stay here. I believe Guthrie, who had been offered Avonmouth some time ago, is afraid to tackle such a big job and has been working to get this instead. I don't want to leave here at all, but Buckie does, and as I couldn't possibly stay here under Guthrie, *moi* must move on too.

Wednesday, 9 May

Avonmouth has, for some reason, been scrapped before it was opened. No one knows why, though some say the ground was so swampy that the foundations of the buildings became unsafe, but I don't know. Anyhow, here we are in Hereford instead.

Quite a different kind of factory – shell-filling picric. Endless raised corridors with roofs, but no sides, and little houses built all along them at distances of about 10 yards. All these have to be patrolled, and we have to wear galoshes all the time.

Besides this we have to see the female workers' passes as they come in, take charge of their food cases, as the canteens are outside the factory compound, also of their jewellery. Then one policewoman has to be always seated at the main entrance of the compound to see that every girl has a 'pass out' before she leaves work – except of course at the end of the shift. If the pass is for a bath, the policewoman must see she is back within half an hour; if it is for the surgery, she must see that the nurse has signed as having seen the girl, etc.

At the end of the shift we keep order on the train and see that the right people get into the right carriages. There are special carriages for men, women, manager, officials, nurses, Women Police and so on. Besides this, in the morning the girls have a free breakfast in the canteen at which we preside. We also conduct the new girls around. A new section is being opened for amatol shell-filling, and from ten to sixty new girls are taken on every day. It is a process.

This is what we have to do:

1. Collect all the candidates in the waiting room.
2. Find Mr Whitehead, if we can, and send the girls in to see him ten

144

at a time. He keeps each batch about twenty minutes or half an hour. There are sometimes 100 of them!

3. Get the passes of the accepted ones and get them to be signed by Mr Dunnet, if and when you can find him.
4. Send away the rejected candidates.
5. Take the accepted ones to the surgery and send them in one at a time to the lady doctor. This takes an age.
6. Send away the rejected ones and return their passes.
7. Take those that passed to have their photograph taken.
8. Take them to the time clock and get a clocking card for each. Show them how to clock.
9. Take them to the section manager, if you can find him, so that he can tell you which are to work at which job, and on which shift.
10. Take them to the change room attendants and get them dressed in 'clean way suits'.
11. Take them to their respective shops to start work.

Sometimes this process takes from 9.00 am till 4.00 pm.

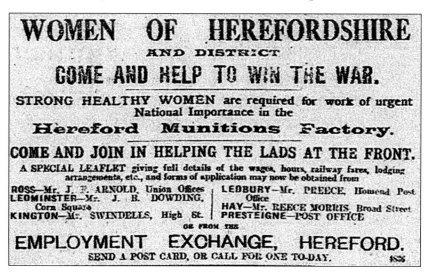

This advertisement appeared in the Hereford Journal *on Saturday, 7 July 1917.*

> **Royal Ordnance Factory, Rotherwas, Hereford**
> The establishment, which covered a 27 acre site, was opened on 11 November 1916 as a factory for filling shells, including some filled with mustard gas. Around 70,000 shells per week were filled. As many as 4,000 of the 6,000 employees were women. It continued as a munitions factory in the Second World War. There is now a Rotherwas group assembling a list of all who were employed there.

Sunday, 10 June

The girls here are really rough and very unruly, simply because they always get their own way, and they know it. Endless rules are made and we have to enforce them. The girls strike and go and yell outside the main office for an hour or two. The manager or his assistant comes out, hears their grievance and says it shall be removed, and it is. They promptly find a new one.

Strikes and rows are more sport than filling shells. We have already had half a dozen strikes, which all ended in the same way.

Two shifting women dismissed – strike – reinstated.

Three girls dismissed for laziness – strike – reinstated.

Girls wish for a rise – strike – rise given.

Girls object to being controlled during their dinner hour or when they leave the plant – strike – now they do what they want.

It is therefore almost impossible to keep any sort of order, because they know they will not be punished for disobeying.

Last week, a girl refused to let me search her. I telephoned the inspector, who went to see the assistant manager, who said the girl was to be turned out of the factory. We turned her out. Other girls rather awestruck. She went down to the manager, wept and said she was sorry etc., and by and by, turned up with a paper to say she was to be allowed back to work. Other girls very cock-a-hoop, of course. In the evening, a box of matches and some cigarettes were found by the charge hand inside an empty shell in that girl's shop. No wonder she wouldn't be searched.

Monday, 18 June

The Women Police all have a weekly drill now. We are drilled by the CO of the Home Defence Corps. It is great sport. When he is not there the sergeants have to do it – most terrifying, at first. Your own voice sounds very peculiar.

At the factory they are very great on fire alarms. The hooter goes and you have to run for your life to the nearest Red Cross on the side of the corridor. There you sound the fire alarm and blow your whistle, and collect all the workers. You wait until the all safe signal is given or the signal that means 'scoot' – in which case, the girls are all to dash for safety the nearest way they can.

Last week at night there was a real fire and a whole shed was burnt. Luckily it was a melt house. If the filled shells had been affected, there wouldn't be much of a factory left. Once they begin to go off, it is all up. When the fire was out and we were busy getting the girls back, one was found still beating the fire alarm, having gone on through the whole performance – a sort of female Casabianca.

Casabianca

Extract from the poem by Felicia Dorothea Hemans, published 1826 and learnt by many school children in Edwardian England.

The boy stood on the burning deck
Whence all but he had fled;
The flame that lit the battle's wreck
Shone round him o'er the dead.

Yet beautiful and bright he stood,
As born to rule the storm;
A creature of heroic blood,
A proud though childlike form.

The poem commemorates a real incident on the ship *Orient* in the Battle of the Nile, when the captain's son refused to leave his post and perished.

After the fire, the Women Police were congratulated on their coolness and good work, Ahem!

Instead of being directly under the orders of the manager as we were at Pembrey, we are here under the Senior DBO [Senior District British

Officer], Colonel Knox Gore. As the manager is a horror and the DBO is a dear, this is a great advantage. Colonel Knox Gore is quite an elderly old gent. He takes great interest in the Women Police, reads the daily report, writes comments on it, speaks to any policewoman he comes across in the factory and does all he can to help us in every way.

One of the junior DBOs is a fearful little puppy. He is very particular about being saluted, and if some unlucky constable should fail to recognize him in his danger building overalls and not salute, she is reported without fail.

We got our own back though the other day. He stopped Sergeant Moore and told her he wished her to tell her constables to salute, and he would like to point out he is not as young as he looks and had been in factory work long before he came here. All this because a newly arrived, very shy policewoman recruit, failed to salute him. Sergeant Moore duly entered in the duty book:

At 11.25 am Lieutenant Gunter Smith informed Sergeant Moore:
1. He wishes to be saluted.
2. He is not as young as he looks.
3. He has been in a factory before.

I can imagine old Knox Gore's chuckles when he read the report.

The Superintendent (Smith), of the Specials employed in the factory, is a little cad, always ready to catch us out, and make fools of us. He was just the same under the previous policewoman, Inspector Champneys. He came into our office one day without knocking and began to bullyrag and sneer at me about some report I'd sent in. Persisted in calling me 'My dear lassie'.

I told him he was a nasty little cad and if he called me that again I'd throw him out of the office. He seemed vastly tickled as he is a tall man and about twice my size. However, he was standing near the door when he called me 'lassie' again. I gave him a sudden shove and banged the door up against him with my other hand, and landed him outside before he knew it. Later, I went down and gave a report of my deed to Colonel Knox Gore and Lieutenant Kingsbury. They began to solemnly put down a long report of the incident, but relapsed into giggles halfway through, so I don't think I shall get into very serious trouble for my breach of discipline.

Wednesday, 4 July

The Amatol section is now working. There are eventually to be seven units, each unit employing 100 girls on each shift. Amatol is made of nitrate of ammonia and TNT pounded and mixed together into a fine pinkish powder. The internal arrangements of a shell are complicated as there are smoke bags, washers, exploder bags and what not to be put in. I won't attempt to describe it as I don't understand it.

The amatol is in some ways more dangerous than the picric. The nitrate of ammonia is dried in a big cylinder, then it and the TNT are put into the mills – things like very old fashioned cyder [*sic*] presses; a trough with a crushing wheel that runs round and round in it. Occasionally, the mixture catches on fire, so each mill has a fireproof cover, drenching tap and fireproof doors to it in case of emergency.

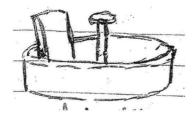

The cyder mill press.

One of them did go off one day and the chargehand pulled the handle of the drencher, drew down the fireproof cover and shut the fire doors of all the sections before leaving. She never got any recognition for this but the supervisor of the truck girls has been given the OBE. There was a tiny fire in one of the picric melt houses, a thing that happens frequently. One of the girls began to cry 'fire', and several charged down the corridor in full flight. The supervisor met them and said, 'Don't be silly. There is no danger,' and quieted them down. There WAS no danger and she was not anywhere near the fire at any time. This just shows what a lottery decorations are.

Monday, 16 July

Last night as I was preparing to go home at about seven o'clock, I found a girl who last week was discharged from the factory hanging round the gates. She refused to go away and said she was sure the factory was going to be blown up etc.

Most of the officials had gone home, so I had to take her to the secretary – an awful old fool. The girl told him she didn't mean no harm and she always went to church every Sunday, and a lot more rubbish. He was most sympathetic and told her to do what the policewoman told her and go away.

Silly old idiot. Of course she didn't go far, and at 10.00 pm, when the night workers came out for dinner, she turned up again. She told all the girls that the factory would be blown up at 3.00 am. None of them would go back to work, but stayed outside in the road in a state of wild excitement. At 3.30 am, the factory not having blown up, they consented to go back to work. The girl has been certified insane and sent to an asylum. So much for the persuasive powers of the secretary.

Thursday, 30 August
I feel a perfect rag. I never had such a week in my life. Some time ago, several lots of Irish girls were taken on to work in the Amatol.

There had been a lot of bad blood between them and the English. The Irish sang Sinn Fein songs and made offensive remarks about the Tommies. The English replied in kind. Each side waxed very wroth. The Irish wore orange and green, the English, red white and blue. This went on for weeks, and Buckie reported to the manager that trouble was brewing. This was pooh-poohed.

Last week, during the dinner hour, an English girl accused an Irish girl of stealing her dinner. The Irish girl replied by spitting in the English girl's face. There was a battle, all the others standing around and cheering on the combatants. We were called in to separate them. We had to lock the Irish girl up in our office as the others wanted to lynch her.

Next evening, scenting trouble, eight or nine of us went down to see the shift train off from Hereford Station. A tremendous battle ensued on the platform between about twenty Irish and the rest of the shift. We got the Irish separated out, one at a time, and put in the waiting room. I stood guard in front of the door, which unfortunately wouldn't shut. Behind me stormed the Irish and in front, the English, until the latter were gradually pushed across to the other platform and got into the train.

Then we let the Irish girls out. They insisted on walking at once to the factory to see the manager, so we walked with them. Crowds of people hooted and threw mud at them. One girl fell and was kicked by a young man in the crowd. I and another policewoman grabbed him and called a policeman who had seen it done, but instead of taking him, the policeman slunk off, so we had to let the man go.

One of the Irish girls was quite beside herself, eyes dull and glassy and face purplish. She burst out every now and then into wild shrieks, and danced and skipped along in front of the others shaking her hands above her head and crying, 'Will we be trampled on? No!' The others tried to calm her a bit but she took no notice whatever; in fact, I don't think she could hear them.

Arrived at the factory and the girls were taken to see the manager. All shrieked at once, but in the end it was settled that they should all be sent back to Ireland the following day. It was arranged that they should be driven back to Hereford so as to avoid further scenes. One of the officials went off to phone for a charabanc. Meanwhile, we attended to the injured. There was a broken head, several cuts, a lot of bruises and a strained wrist. At 9.30 pm, the charabanc had not arrived.

The English girls were due to come out for their dinner hour and trouble would certainly ensue. On enquiring, it was found that the official who went to telephone was so agitated that he forgot about it! The chara was wildly telephoned for and arrived at 9.55 pm. The Irish were bundled in and had just disappeared when the shift came out for dinner.

Next morning, the Irish girls were put into reserved carriages and sent off to Ireland. The Herefordians assembled on the embankments, as they were not allowed into the station, and pelted the train with rotten vegetables, eggs and bad language.

So ended the Irish rebellion.

[There is no account of this in the local papers except in the *Hereford Journal*. On 11 August 1917, in an article about a busy bank holiday, there is the phrase, 'Notwithstanding a large exodus of factory girls'.]

Sunday, 2 September

Another rumpus. Two policewomen were walking home one night when a terrified girl came running up, begging for protection, because she said some girls were after her, threatening to murder her.

Presently up came a yelling pack, crying out that they would skin her alive and so on. There was a tussle, but some men came to the rescue and the aggressors withdrew. The policewomen escorted the intended victim home.

She left Hereford next day. Apparently, she was a charge hand who had reported two girls for slacking and had got them dismissed. They and their friends had set out to be revenged in this way.

About a month or so ago, five or six girls set on a sergeant of the Women Police, knocked her down, spoilt her hat and so on. Although she and two others were prepared to swear to two of the worst offenders, these were not dismissed, only reprimanded! Naturally, one can't keep much order under these circumstances.

Sunday, 9 September

A great and terrible strike, as usual, for more pay and less work. The girls stormed around, yelled, shrieked, threw mud and so on. Then they discovered a wretched little creature who had dared to come to work.

Being timekeeper's clerk and not in the sheds at all, she really had known nothing about the strike. She was well scared, though. They chased her from one end of the factory to another, and she fled for protection to the policewoman's office.

The strikers threw water and knocked down a policewoman who prevented them from getting the 'blackleg'.

The men police eventually came out and helped drive them away. Then they [the strikers] went to the main office and broke all the windows, demanding to see the manager. He said he wouldn't see them until they were quiet. Major Dobson, CO of the Home Defence, got out the fire hose and began to squirt the strikers, but it burst. Eventually, they were tired out and went home, and appear now to have forgotten all about it.

I never knew such an unruly wild set of hooligans in my life.

The new Amatol girls are at the bottom of all the trouble. They are recruited in batches of twenty to a hundred; some come from the Midlands, some from Yorkshire, Ireland, Scotland and Wales. They are brought down here and, if accepted, put into very rough hostels or cheap lodgings. Naturally under those circumstances, only the roughest of the rough will come, and a good many are girls that have come away from home because they had made things too hot for themselves. Anyhow, they are a great trial. They steal like magpies, fight, get up scandalous tales about each other, strike, and do their best to paint things red.

Monday, 10 September

For some time, Buckie has been trying to get away from Hereford. The picric acid makes her ill and she has had several gastric attacks. Also, it is rather disheartening to work under a manager who is constantly inventing new rules for us to enforce, but does not back us up by punishing those who disobey them.

But the real reason is that Buckie has been fighting to get us sworn in. In a factory like this, where we have a good deal of genuine police work to do (i.e. prosecuting for bringing in matches, for theft, blackmail, etc. and our work during strikes and riots), it is really important that we should have the power to take out and serve a summons and carry through a case without being obliged to pass everything over to the men police.

Buckie was promised that we should be sworn in, but some hitch has occurred, so she has now said if we are not sworn in she will resign. We have not been and so she has resigned, and has been appointed by Headquarters Sub Inspector of Waltham Abbey Royal Gunpowder and Royal Small Arms Factories.

As an instance of the importance of being sworn in, during the strike the girls attacked a policeman and knocked off his helmet, and also knocked down a policewoman. For assaulting the police they were liable to six months' hard labour. Assaulting the policewoman counted only as common assault, as we not being sworn in count as private individuals, and the maximum penalty is one month.

Tuesday, 2 October
Have also been transferred to Waltham, and I arrived at Paddington to find an air raid in progress. At 6.00 pm, no porters to be had. Eventually, the All Clear was sounded and I secured a very doddery and frightened old gentleman who succeeded in losing some of my luggage. After finding it again, I could not get a cab for love nor money, so had to take my luggage back to the cloakroom. On the way, the Take Cover sounded again, and the old chap was petrified with fright. However, I managed to get the things in. Going out of the station, a taxi literally hailed me. I scrambled in and went back to the cloakroom for my luggage. I had Rip, numerous boxes, two bikes and various hampers. The driver, to my astonishment, made no fuss but drove me and mine through an air raid to Liverpool Street Station. He then explained matters by saying he had been a policeman himself once!

I was told to change at Stratford. When we got there all the lights went out. I got out and was gently taken by the hand by a porter and led through the subway and into another train. We stopped several times and there was a lot of firing and Verey lights.

At Waltham no one could direct me, so I rode without lights, about 2 miles, and managed by good luck to arrive at my destination, the matron's hostel. Buckie came back from the factory at 1.00 am, when the All Clear sounded.

Saturday, 20 October
I haven't had an instant to write up my diary owing to the constant air raids. We had five in quick succession after my arrival. It is not necessary to describe them all, but perhaps my first experience of a raid when on duty may be interesting.

The hooters sounded at about 6.30 pm, before the girls' supper hour. Buckie went to one end of the factory and I to the other. There are no real shelters for the girls, who have to leave the danger sheds and crouch under the cleanways. These are the raised gangways that lead from one shed to another. The ground underneath is often very wet and covered with nettles; also there are sometimes rats, and always plenty of slugs. These small matters make it extremely difficult to get the girls to go under cover, and still more difficult to keep them there.

In my part of the factory there were two batches of girls to be looked after, divided from each other by a ten-minute walk. As I had only been round the factory once, in daylight, I found it almost impossible to find my way at night, with all the lights out. The girls were very quiet and only two or three seemed at all frightened, but it was horribly cold and everyone was starving by the time the All Clear went, and several girls were ill from the combined effects of cold, damp and want of food.

The Women Police here are most fearfully undisciplined. The inspector who is leaving appears to have been a very nice woman, but with no idea of organizing, rather inclined to listen to talebearers and far too kind in her dealings, with the result that she got herself ducked in a small pond inside the factory by one of the policewomen.

The two sergeants now here are also leaving, one out of sympathy for the inspector and the other because she has been offered promotion. There are twelve policewomen left, but so far only two or three turn up for duty at one time, and the afternoon constables generally don't come at all, either because they are afraid of being caught in an air raid or because, owing to raids, their London trains do not run. Nearly all come from London, but funnily enough, the night I came down from London, no other constables turned up because 'none of the trains ran.'

The factory is very straggling. It is (including Royal Small Arms Enfield) about 7 miles long and only 1¼ miles wide. We have three offices dotted about in the RGPF [Royal Gunpowder Factory] and one in the RSGF [sic: she means the RSAF, Royal Small Arms Factory]. The constables allotted to the various beats go at once to the nearest office to that beat and work from there for the rest of the day. This means that it is not possible for the sergeant to see every constable as she comes to work. Inspector Coates had no means of knowing if a constable came punctually or not, but now they are made to clock in.

They also had an ingenious system of persuading the men police to ring them up when Inspector Coates was seen to leave her office and start on her rounds. Until they received this phone message, they would sit in the various offices, leaving the factory to look after itself. This little trick has also been circumvented. Also, a night shift has been started. There was none before because the constables said they couldn't manage it! The result was there was no one in charge of the factory girls at night or in air raids unless one or two of the afternoon policewomen happened to get caught, and this they took care shouldn't happen often.

I am rather surprised that in a place so near London, the chiefs should have allowed the Women Police to get into such an undisciplined state. Apparently, it wasn't until the ducking of the inspector brought things to a head that they did anything to right the matter.

During one of the recent raids, five incendiary bombs fell in the factory. One fell on the wooden platform in front of the cordite press houses and went out, one fell against the door of the blank cutting and burnt part of the paint off, one fell in front of a policeman and 'knocked him into the river', in other words, jumped him into the river [or he jumped!], and two fell on marshy bits of ground and buried themselves.

The factory is very beautiful. The land is flat, but thickly wooded. Two branches of the river Lee flow through it, and the whole is cut up by hundreds of canals and cuts. Every house has a door opening on to the water, and all the explosives are carried from one section of the factory to another by water. The 'gunpowder boats' look like houseboats on a small scale, with rounded tops, and are pulled by eight or nine men.

A 'gunpowder boat'.

These men wear a rather picturesque uniform consisting of a canvas garment exactly the shape of an old leather jerkin, little black peaked caps like jockeys, and baggy black knee breeches and leather leggings.

The girls' uniform is also pretty. It varies a little according to the work they do, but most wear knickers, and tunic and red caps. The tunic and knees of the knickers are tied with red laces, buttons being forbidden. Many of the girls wear coloured stockings as the uniforms are very neatly cut. They look very charming.

But to continue my description of the factory itself:

The houses being far apart and the ground between them well wooded, it is extraordinarily quiet and lonely. The ground too is very damp, so that few people venture off the beaten tracks. There are all kinds of fish in the water, which is very clear. There are also lots of flowers and ponds full of lilies. In one part there was once a garden and there are still roses, raspberries etc. growing there. There are numbers of water hens and I have also seen rabbits, rats, stoats, grass snake, dragonflies galore, quantities of pheasant, a swan, kingfishers and an otter. Also, wild duck. It is most delightful having to patrol in such a lovely place with so many interesting flowers and beasties around.

The making of gunpowder has been carried on here by the government for 200 years. They bought it from John Walton, brother of Isaac Walton, and before that, it had been in existence for a great number of years, some say since the time of Elizabeth, and one policewoman assured me, since the time of Harold! Some of the sheds now in use were standing in the time of John Walton and are very picturesque red brick with red tiled roofs.

One part of the factory, which goes by the name of Daisy Island, is said to be the site of a hunting lodge belonging to Henry VIII to which he sent Anne Boleyn when he had had enough of her. There is a little shed on one of the islands in which a Bible was always kept for the benefit of the night watchman. On one of the walls dividing 'Nitroglycerine' from 'Cordite', there is an inscription:

> Evil like a trickling stream can be damned with ease at the source, but once let it become a flowing stream and not philosophy, nary nor religion will serve to stem the flood.

This noble sentiment was carved on the wall by order of a certain gentleman who was in the habit of fishing in the factory in pre-war days.

One evening, we were awakened by a whizz and a bang, and rushed up to the factory to find that two of the cordite stores were on fire. The flames rose to a tremendous height. Almost immediately, the Take Cover was sounded, but luckily a heavy mist came down and I suppose hid the flames from the enemy. Anyway, though they came quite near, they didn't drop any bombs. It was rumoured that the cordite was set alight by spies as a mark for the aircraft.

Another time during a raid, the sky became quite light, although there was no moon. Later, there was a rosy glow all over the northern horizon. Everyone thought the Germans must have started some huge fire at Cambridge, or somewhere in that direction. The only person who didn't agree was a policeman, who continued to repeat; 'I don't know what it is but it isn't a fire; that I do know.'

Later, there were flashes of silvery fire and a sort of gold shimmering. The policeman was right. It wasn't a fire, but the Great Northern Lights. The first time I've ever seen them.

The girls are very plucky during a raid, and really very good tempered too, considering the cold and discomfort of a raid. There are now shelters of a kind. They are called 'dugouts', but there is no digging about them. They are little huts made of packing cases, with a few sandbags and brushwood on the roof. Each dugout holds eight to twelve girls, and they have the advantage of keeping the girls divided into small groups, thus preventing stampedes and panics, and they also do protect from flying shrapnel, though of course they would be useless against bombs or unexploded shells. The girls, however, are fully convinced they are shell-proof.

A dugout shelter.

It is our duty to cram the girls into these little objects and to keep them there. Also, to go round and round from one to the other cheering up the occupants etc. It becomes very cold and monotonous after an hour or two.

We – Buckie and I – are now living in a cottage at the factory gate. A very nice comfy cottage, too. There are three bedrooms, two sitting rooms and a back kitchen, so we have a lodger in the second sitting room.

May 1918
Quite a big explosion. Recently, a new machine has been put in for waterproofing the guncotton. In the middle of the night it blew up. Two girls were working it. The shed was wrecked and the machine blown to chips, and the girls shot out into the bank opposite. One found that her shoes were alight so calmly kicked them off, and both trotted up to the canteen. Meanwhile, agitated firemen were hunting for their dismembered remains.

Afterword

And there the diaries end. There clearly was at least one more little black notebook. On the opposite page of the final volume, outline jottings exist for the next one.

This is what she wrote:

> Wages at Enfield.
> J.B.D.
> Library, Dracula.
> Rip and the wall.
> Air raid. Joan. Cake.
> Abbey.

All one can be is frustrated at the stories we have missed.

Somewhere in the sixty years between the last entry at the end of 1917 and 1979, when the diaries finally were deposited at the Imperial War Museum, any remaining instalments were lost. Many things could have happened in sixty years to those insignificant, little 6 inch by 4 inch notebooks that held such an interesting story.

They might have never have made it back from India, where Bobby's favourite brother and recipient of the diaries remained until well after the end of the war. They might simply have got overlooked and thrown away in the many removals that took place over the years.

We do have some idea of what happened to Bobby after 1917. In 1979, as a result of having given the diaries to the IWM, aged eighty-nine, she was interviewed twice on tape. As always, from this distance the listener is exasperated by the questions never asked. It is easy to be wise after the event. Both interviews are occasionally interrupted by the barking of her the little dog of that time.

Some of her comments, made with the hindsight of sixty years, and after having been through a second world war, are interesting:

Q. Did you hate the Germans?
A. I think we hated them, in theory, anyway. We heard lurid

stories, but I don't think we really believed them. But after the last war, we've been obliged to believe something these days, haven't we?

Q. Did you see the Zeppelin air raids?

A. Oh yes, but air raids in those days were nothing to what they are today.

She talks of seeing the Zeppelin 'that was brought down by a new type of bullet', which was intended to ignite the gas. She says, 'We saw the underneath of it, which was carrying the personnel, burn and drop off. They were all killed, of course. It was dreadful. They never came back.'

The reader will wonder what happened to her immediately after the diaries finish. We know from the recordings that she continued working at the Royal Ordnance Factory, Enfield, in the factory police until the end of the war.

In the 1979 interview she is asked about the Armistice. She says, 'We all knew it was coming for some days, before it was signed. There were sirens. The uproar was tremendous.'

She goes on, 'A few weeks after the Armistice, we were told our services were no longer required. They did say they would try and find us work. And that was the end of that. But I never asked them to find me a job.'

We know, partly from her own account and partly from family legend, that for a while she and a friend ran a tea room in Chepstow on the Wye. It was called the Why Not.

'It was quite the thing to do then and we did very comfortably for some years. Eventually, we sold it.'

Bobby lived to be a hundred and never married. She once answered my little sister's question by saying, 'Well, men were a little thin on the ground then.'

Many women of her generation didn't marry. Though there is much discussion as to actual percentages and numbers, it is accepted that a disproportionate number of men of the UK middle classes died in the First World War.

A frequently quoted statistic is that, whereas 12 per cent of the enlisted men died, 17 per cent of the officer class did. Another statement often heard is that one third of the Oxford University class of 1913 died on the battlefields.

AFTERWORD

Of course, many more enlisted men died than did officers, but it seems clear that the loss was disproportionally greater among officers, who were of course the intended husbands of the Gabrielle Wests of that generation and class.

In the 1920s, much was made of what was referred to as the 'Surplus Woman'. Most recently, Virginia Nicholson, in her book *Singled Out,* details the constant public discussion about 'a million women too many'.

Whatever the truth of the statistics, and there is an argument that says that there was a shortage of middle-class marriageable men even before the war, it is undoubtedly true that a generation of women born after 1890 believed they would have difficulty finding a suitable husband.

I offer two literary comments on the public debate at the time. The first is Vera Brittain's poem, *The Superflous Woman.*

The Superfluous Woman
Ghosts crying down the vistas of the years,
Recalling words
Whose echoes have long died,
And kind moss grown
Over the sharp and blood-bespattered stones
Which cut our feet in ancient ways.

But who will look for my coming?

Long busy days when many meet and part;
Crowded aside
Remembered hours of hope;
And city streets
Grown dark and hot with eager multitudes
Hurrying homeward whither response waits.

But who will seek me at nightfall?

Light fading where the chimneys cut the sky;
Footsteps that pass,
Nor tarry at my door.
And far away,

161

MENUS, MUNITIONS AND KEEPING THE PEACE

Behind the row of crosses, shadows black
Stretch out long arms before the mouldering sun.

But who will give me my children?

Vera Brittain, 1919

The second is an excerpt from Dorothy L. Sayers' mystery novel, *Unnatural Death*, published in 1927. Her hero, Lord Peter Wimsey, is presumably voicing his creator's sentiments when talking about the enquiry agency he has just set up, staffed entirely by women, when he says:

> Miss Climpson is a manifestation of the wasteful way this country is run. ... Thousands of old maids bursting with useful energy forced by our stupid social system into hydros and hotels. ... One of these days they will put up a statue to me with an inscription:

To the Man who Made
Thousands of Superfluous Women
Happy
without Injury to their Modesty
or Execution to Himself

This was the early twentieth century. It was still true that no woman of Bobby's background would have married without her father's consent, and no socially aspirational clergyman father with money troubles was going to allow his daughter to marry beneath her, out of her class.

There is one more insight into her single state. It is found in the interview, as a comment on a story she tells about her time at the Woolwich Arsenal Canteen.

In the entry for 8 April 1916, Bobby writes of cooking breakfast every morning for the engineering assistant, who in return for having his sausages and gammon cooked, gives Bobby chocolates. 'And very nice too,' she writes.

In 1979, she added to this story: 'My father was very shocked at my going to Woolwich, which was a bad part of London, and at the canteen work, too. He watched me and one day somehow penetrated to the

Gabrielle West with her great-nieces Julia and Sarah (Avalon Weston, the editor, on Gabrielle's left) in Dorset in the 1950s.

canteen. I can't think how, as strangers weren't allowed in. He thought it was a romantic affair, but it was purely a matter of sausages and beef steak. He thought it was a very bad business.'

It is, of course, possible that her parents had always regarded her as the younger daughter whose job it was going to be to stay home and care for her elderly parents.

Bobby certainly believed this was her destiny. Again in the 1979 interview, when asked what she did after the tea room was sold, she said, 'My parents were getting older and needed me.' There is a poignant entry in July 1914, just before the war has started: 'Sunday afternoon, went out for a walk. Nothing but couples. Came home again.'

It is followed by a drawing, across two pages, of five couples hand in hand.

Bobby spent the best part of the next forty years as a carer for one relative or another. When the companion of her retirement years developed dementia, she visited her every day in her care home until she died.

The writer came to know her Aunt Bobby in the mid-1950s. She had her own house in Dorset and invited her fatherless great-nieces to stay for a couple of summer holidays.

In those days she and her companion had two little dogs, unclipped poodles. She also, rented a big beach hut on the sands for our stay. To my sister and myself, London city children, this was just amazing. We could change into our swimsuits, have picnics, build sandcastles and stay out all day on the sands. I remember being sad when told we couldn't sleep there because it wasn't allowed by law.

Bobby did her best with these two shy but wild, damaged small girls. In reality, she did prefer her dogs. Nevertheless, the possession of a house actually on the beach meant to us she was a really splendid aunt.

She was, for many years, a member of the Bournemouth Natural Science Society, and according to family legend, is credited with discovering a particular orchid growing in her part of Dorset.

In retrospect, the greatest tragedy for Bobby was that, unlike her brothers or her elder sister, she wasn't allowed a sound education, nor did she ever gain any qualifications.

As we have seen, she was a formidable organizer. Today, she might well have been a senior civil servant, a parish priest in her own right, or even a bishop. Perhaps she might have run her own business or a famous multinational company. In her own time, she would have made a dedicated headmistress, and possibly a better academic or a farmer.

With a proper education she might have had a chance in her long life to make other contributions to her generation's wellbeing, thus adding to the many made by that distinguished 'monstrous regiment' of 'surplus' women.

There is a long list of their contributions, but many of this author's generation just remember them as their schoolteachers, the hospital matrons who trained them as nurses and the stalwarts of every church community and civic society.

Aunt Bobby may have been denied an education, but the First World War gave her the big adventure that maybe we all need. The under-occupied, rather cross, too energetic young woman of July 1914 was challenged, and discovered her strengths. For the rest of her life she had memories. She didn't become a bad-tempered old maid. She looked after a long line of needy relatives, watched the world go by and told the stories of her adventures to, among others, this great-niece.

Her adventure gave us the diaries, written before those women knew they would be considered 'superfluous'. These insignificant little notebooks have endured, and now published, their contents will be available for all to read. They provide a detailed and fascinating account of one woman's war and her brief escape from patriarchy.

When in 1979, some sixty years later, she was asked as a final interview question whether she enjoyed her First World War work, she replied with the dignified enthusiasm of one aged eighty-nine, reflecting on a past of long ago, 'Very much. It was very interesting.'

*   *   *

I would like to add two postscripts to this commentary.

Firstly, there is a small irony in the family history. It involved Bobby's father's death. As we know, wherever she went, Bobby's bicycle went too. Her father, the Reverend G.H. West, died aged eighty-two in 1927, some days after being knocked down by a bicycle. There was an inquest and in the local newspaper it is reported that the two of Bobby's brothers present, Charles and George, go to great lengths to exonerate the cyclist from any blame. The third brother, the  diary recipient Michael, was still in India, and her mother's diary reports that Bobby couldn't be spared from the tea shop to attend.

Secondly, Rip, Bobby's terrier, has featured often in these diaries. Even when not mentioned, he was always with her. Aunt Bobby continued to have small dogs right up until her death. In her will, made in 1989, when she was ninety-nine, the year before she died, the last paragraph makes provision for her final pet dog:

> I place on record that Mrs Owen has instructions as to my little dog and <u>DIRECT</u> that any charges in connection therewith shall be paid from my estate.

Bobby's beloved dog, Rip.

Appendix 1

A Victorian Childhood
by Joan Mary West

I am a Victorian, born in 1883, in the reign of the good old queen, whom we then venerated. In fact, I remember getting rather mixed up about the first hymn I learnt. I sang 'children all should be, good, obedient, meek as she'.

'No,' says Mother, '"he".'

'Well,' says I, 'which did you mean? Victoria or Jesus?'

I think those lessons I learned from my mother remain clearer in my mind than much that I learned later. That rather bears out what a great headmaster of Eton once said: 'What a child learns before he is seven will remain with him all his life.' And it also corroborates the old saying 'The hand that rocks the cradle rules the world'. Well, the old queen might not have rocked the cradle much, but she certainly ruled the world in our youth, in more ways than one. She set a very definite standard of decorum in the court, reflections of which descended even to the nursery, our schoolroom and our books, in matters of behaviour.

I was talking of hymns. Have you ever noticed in your *Ancient and Modern* hymnbook that some of the best known are accredited to Canon Twells? Well, every Bournemouth child knew him – dear, gnome-like, ugly old man, a face like a wrinkled walnut, a thatch of untidy grey hair, huge nose and two brilliant eyes, a large mobile mouth: and when that old man smiled at a child, the child would remember it all his life. His parties were red letter days.

How well I remember being dressed in fine muslin, all-over embroidery and flounces, a skirt about 6 inches long, sticking out like a ballerina's, little white satin shoes, all covered with beads, and with short silk socks. My short hair was done over a long stick in two sausages (as Father called them) down the middle of my head – the finishing touch, which I loathed. Nan would come when the nursemaid had me ready and put on my shoulder ribbons. They were passed inside my short sleeves by Nan's cold fingers – ugh! – and tied on each shoulder. Then a string of beads to match, and a great watered-silk wide sash with a bow behind. White coats for me and the three brothers, and off we went in an old Scotts four-wheeler that had a queer smell of hay and horse and stuffiness that always made me feel ill.

That old cab came from a rank near our church. And I can see now the decorous old butler from old Lady C.'s home opposite the rank, staggering out on frosty mornings with huge jugs of hot tea for the cabbies. That old lady was a rather prim old stick with a heart of gold. If you called when she didn't want to appear, the old butler would say: 'Her Ladyship *is* at home but she is not receiving.'

She would use the conventional 'not at home' if she was.

Well, that brings me, as it were, to the church, St Swithin's, and the Victorian Sunday, which I looked upon as good in parts, like the curate's egg. On Sundays, when we were old enough, we had a nine o'clock breakfast with the parents – lovely buttered eggs and a big silver egg on a stand that held half a pound of butter and opened when you turned a knob. The big silver kettle with blue-flamed spirit lamp underneath, which bent forward and poured when you undid a chain at the back. There was always the hope that the spirit lamp would boil over – or Mother undo the wrong chain and upset the whole kettle, and cause what was to *me* a joyous confusion.

Then church: all the boys of our school in Etons in front, punctuated by a master at the end of each row. Fat Mrs Wells, the matron – or Mrs Swells, as the boys called her – in front of Mother, and then all of us. At the end of the rows, all the beautiful shiny toppers piled on top of each other on the pipes. I remember relieving the tedium of the litany by tweaking at them and collapsing the whole pile. I dined in the nursery that day!

Well, after church, a walk along the cliff, where one met everyone all in Sunday rig. In summer, for me, a deyhorn hat with buttercups and daisies: the same in spring with ostrich feathers that had to be re-curled each time there was damp in the air. Nan threw brown sugar on the fire, and held the feather in the smoke, then curled it over the blade of a knife. On windy days, how I loathed that hat, always blowing off, or over one's nose. In winter, we all three wore white fur coats and caps, and the grown-ups called us 'the three bears'. Everyone kissed us everywhere – so tiresome. They went into raptures or hysterics over George, who always went barefoot because he would not wear anything on his feet. I tried it, because it attracted so much attention, but decided it was not worth the discomfort.

After church parade came dinner with parents, in the little panelled private dining room. I remember the white cloth and red glass jugs at each corner. Red, because the former plain glass ones acted as magnifiers, and one hot day set up a little bonfire in each corner. There were the darns to remind us of the thrill. We each had christening mugs in which to drink ginger beer – and lots to eat, followed by dessert on plates decorated with life-size fruits. Then finger bowls to rinse in afterwards. There is a replete and fizzy feeling always connected with Sunday afternoons in my mind.

The children's service was at 3.00 pm and then drawing room tea. We had a set of miniature chairs and tables in the bay window, a tea set decorated all over with maidenhair fern. If any of us behaved badly, the privy punch, the wild unseemly yell, Mother would just quietly pull the long embroidered bell-pull. When the parlour maid appeared, she would say: 'Master or Miss So-and-so would like to go up to the nursery, Jane, so will you ask Nurse to come?' Nan would then glide over the floor and remove the offender. Should he battle or yell (Mike usually did), no eruption ever upset the even order of her going, as if she went on castors. You were silently engulfed and removed as she glided from the room!

Our toys were kept in an alcove, one side for weekday drawing room occupations, the other for Sunday – puzzles, texts, and a frame with removable back containing a picture for each Sunday of the year. The one we really liked was Daniel in the lion's den, and his turn was ages coming round. In winter, from November to Christmas, we made the crèche, and this we loved. It involved glue-potting and cutting out. A Chinese idol from the curiosity cupboard had to be a Magi, because he had no legs, so looked as though he was kneeling. We also made a model of the Tabernacle, and oh, the trouble we had over the sacrificial lamb! He would stick his legs in the air and none of us could bring himself to tweak them. The day we dyed the curtains for the Holy of Holies – after singing a hymn about it – was a glory day, particularly when George went and upset the basin and it went all over the rug!

One Christmas, the crèche caught fire. We were quite pleased because it meant collecting all the items over again, with visits to Beal's toyshops.

Charles said it should have been the Tabernacle (i.e. that caught fire) because then it would have been a real burnt offering sacrifice! We sold that model for £4 at the C.M.S. Exhibition.

There were one or two parties on a grand scale. I remember a garden party we gave, with Punch and Judy and a donkey, and a goat-cart hired from the beach: and going down to the great dark kitchen to see Cook icing cakes by the yard. Mother had a 'den', as it was called, a little room leading out of the anteroom into the drawing room. In the ante were marble consol [*sic*] tables with huge bronze vases, and dragons in full relief on them. They rather scared me at night, as they almost seemed to move in the dim light of a coloured glass lantern. Mother did all her hobbies in the den. She had the chef from Gattes in the arcade to teach her cake icing. The cake was kept under a bell glass, and more festoons added each week. One day, Mother forgot to put back the bell glass and in the morning, there was a hole in the side of the cake, a neat pile of fruit-like miniature cannon balls beside it – and inside, no cake at all!

I only remember Mother trying to teach me to read once. Nan must have been ill. We did A, then B. Mother showed me a Bee with a picture. Blank. 'This is Bee,' said Mother. 'Can't be,' I said. 'If that letter is B, how can Bee be the same? Must be a bluebottle.'

Mother taught us the Bible and our duty to charity. So much of our pocket money had to go to this – and a yearly visit to take a doll to an orphanage. No sugar in Lent, and the proceeds to a mission. And, at the age of twelve, a dress allowance and an account book with a list of what I could afford on each item. I remember being reprimanded for spending 2/6d on a belt! A very nice one it was too, and lasted for years.

To return to lessons: we had a kindergarten. I still retain the miniature chair I sat on when three years old. One or two items I remember – like pinching the doctor's son. He had a big nose and yelled for nothing. Alec Ross (now retired housemaster of Sherborne) was just by himself at the window with beads to string. He spent a profitable half hour flipping them at my mother's pigeons. We had a huge lead tray full of sand (I put some down Alec's neck). I learned about volcanoes made with sand and erupted with a matchbox.

After that I had a series of nursery governesses. The pretty ones never stayed long – they talked to the masters. Then I went to the boys' school for my lessons and we came down and played football and brigands. I once shared a desk with Gladstone's grandson – he was too good to be true. I tried to teach him to drop chalk into his inkwell and then:

'Please, Sir, can I have the duster, Sir, the ink has run over.'

And, two minutes later:

'Please, Sir, can I borrow some blotch paper to mop up my ink? It's run into my Latin Primer.'

I played football with nibs on the top of the desk, and learnt *Albertus ignotus puer non amabat letteras* – but not my tables. Our navy class master went on to Osborne, and meeting him years later, I said:

'Mr I.T., did you ever teach another girl?'

'Heaven forbid!' he said.

I couldn't join the dormitory feasts but I heard all about them – and about the little boy who was hurriedly tumbled into a big trunk and shoved under the bed when my father went on his rounds.

After being educated at the boys' school, my godmother thought I was becoming a tomboy so I was sent to a select girls' school to learn to be a little lady. There was a dancing class at which I did not shine. We marched round and round in white dresses and sandals with books on our heads and tried to look like the ladies in Burne Jones's *Golden Staircase*. Then we had to enter the room one by one, fling the door impressively open, enter and close it behind us without turning our backs (so that you'd have shut it on the nose of anyone happening to be behind). Then you passed along a line of sixty school mates bowing in turns. The thing was to see how many you could include in one bow without accelerating your walk. Why you were expected to meet all your friends in a string I never understood (unless it was to try it out for Sunday parade on the cliff). But some of us would one day be presented, so we had to learn a court curtsey. Three chairs were put out and designated as the Queen, the Prince of Wales etc. We entered and did a curtsey to the floor to each. The solemnity of this – curtseying to empty chairs – always made me giggle, and that usually upset my balance.

Another exercise was to enter, advance to the pianoforte, and sit gracefully, draping your imaginary train, removing your long gloves and smiling pleasantly round, then lay your hands on the keyboard with swan-like wrists! But we also had to learn to sew coats, do First Aid (quite a new idea in those days) and write to the butcher. We played a fierce game of hockey, had three all-England players in our eleven, in fact, and beat the redoubtable Bournemouth 4:0 OK. But we played in scarlet flannel blouses, lined with white flannelette to minimize the risk of cold – though I was nearer apoplexy sometimes.

To improve our figure we 'arched' or shot with bow and arrow. And I, having an old and much too powerful bow, managed with mighty effort to pull it so hard that I very nearly shot the milkman – some feat when you have to stand with your waist in and the other side of your anatomy out and full: you try it!

There was only one (privileged) day girl, the doctor's daughter from Christchurch, 3 miles away. She came on a cushion-tyre bicycle. Our headmistress, after seeing her arrival, requested her never again to appear on that vulgar machine. But within a year, we were all mounted on pneumatic tyres, invented by Mr Dunlop, and rode decorously, two by two, in scarlet blouses and blue skirts, into Boscombe to Battle. The crocodile on bikes!

Written in 1948 for a Women's Institute talk

Appendix 2

Family members and connections mentioned in, or relevant to, Gabrielle
Mary West's diaries.

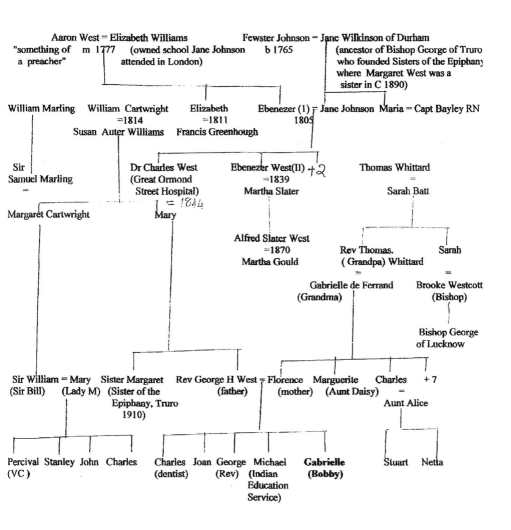

Appendix 3

The Children's Games

The children's singing games that Bobby sent to her brother Michael in India, which he intended to use in his English teaching there, are transcribed below. They might be of interest, a hundred years later.

The Old Woman and the Pig and *The Crooked Man* appear in Iona and Peter Opie's *Oxford Nursery Rhyme Book*.

Please Mother Buy me a Milking Pail is clearly another version of *There's a Hole in my Bucket*, to the same tune, but with a less elegant ending.

Owls and Oysters was probably used in elocution classes, to which many middle-class children were sent to eliminate their local accents.

The version of *Cock Robin* as a game resembles *Poor Jenny is a Weeping*, with less sentiment and more violence!

*   *   *

Extract from the diary:

> You said you wanted some of the children's songs etc., so I am sending you some.
>
> In *The Old Woman and the Pig* you mount up repeating the chorus and adding one extra line each time.

The Old Woman and the Pig

There was once an old woman and she bought a pig at the market,
On the way home they came to a style, and the pig would not get
  over.
So the old woman said:
'Pig, pig, get over the style or I shan't get home tonight.'
But the pig wouldn't.

APPENDIX 3

So she went a little further and she came to a dog, and she said:
'Dog, dog, bite pig. Pig, pig, get over the style or I shan't get
home tonight.'
And the pig wouldn't.

So she went a little further and she found a stick, and she said:
'Stick, stick, beat dog. Dog, dog, bite pig' etc.
But the stick wouldn't.

So she went a little further and found a fire, and she said:
'Fire, fire, burn stick. Stick, stick, beat dog' ... etc.
But the fire wouldn't.

So she went a little further and found some water, and she said:
'Water, water, quench the fire' ... etc.
But the water wouldn't.

So she went a little further and found an ox, and said:
'Ox, ox, drink water. Water, water, quench fire' ... etc.
But the ox wouldn't.

So she went a little further and found a butcher, and said:
'Butcher, butcher, kill ox' ... etc.
But the butcher wouldn't.

So she went a little further and found a rope, and said:
'Rope, rope, hang butcher' ... etc.
But the rope wouldn't.

So she went a little further and found a rat, and said:
'Rat, rat, gnaw rope' ... etc.
But the rat wouldn't.

So she went a little further and found a cat, and said:
'Cat, cat, kill rat,
'Rat, rat, gnaw rope,
'Rope, rope, hang butcher,
'Butcher, butcher, kill ox,

'Ox, ox, drink water,
'Water, water, quench fire,
'Fire, fire, burn stick,
'Stick, stick, beat dog,
'Dog, dog, bit pig,
'Pig, pig, get over the style, or we shan't get home tonight.'

And the cat said:
'Go to the farm and get me some milk.'
So she went to the farm and said to the cow:
'Please, cow, give me some milk,' and the cow said:
'Give me some hay.'
And she went to the haystack and got her some hay,
And the cow gave her the milk
And she took it to the cat,
And ...
The cat began to kill the rat,
The rat began to gnaw the rope,
The rope began to hang the butcher,
The butcher began to kill the ox,
The ox began to drink the water,
The water began to quench the fire,
The fire began to burn the stick,
The stick began to beat the dog,
The dog began to bite the pig,
And the little pig jumped over the style and the old woman got
    home that night.

This is one of the old things Nan used to teach us:

One Old Owl Eating Oysters

Two tall toads totally tired trying to trot to Silbury,
Three thin tailors twisting twenty threaded twine,
Four fat friars fanning fainting fleas,
Five finnicking Frenchmen fricasseeing frogs,
Six solemn students studying scientific saws,
Seven Severn salmon swallowing simple shrimp,

Eight elegantly educated Englishmen examining Europe,
Nine nice neat nimble noblemen nibbling nonpareils,
Ten tall tigers taking tea,
Eleven Eastern elephants entering Europe,
Twelve typographers, typographically transcribing type.

There Was a Crooked Man

There was a crooked man
And he walked a crooked mile
And he found a crooked sixpence
Upon a crooked style
And he bought a crooked cat
That caught a crooked mouse
And they all lived together
In a crooked little house.

Please Mother, Buy me a Milking Pan

Please, Mother, buy me a milking pan,
A milking pan,
A milking pan,
Please, Mother, buy me a milking pan,
A razzum, a tazzum, a lizzurn a tee.

Where can I get the money from? ... etc.
Why don't you sell Father's feather bed? ... etc.
What would Father sleep upon? ... etc.
Sleep in the pigsty ... etc.
Where would the pigs sleep? ... etc.
Why, sleep in the wash tub ... etc.
What could I wash in? ... etc.
Wash in your thimble ... etc.
Thimble isn't big enough ... etc.
Then wash by the riverside ... etc.
Supposing I was to fall in? ... etc.
Yah!

This is a sort of action song in which they all stand round the one who lies on the ground as Cock Robin, while one other stands out till verse three, when she comes in as the old woman. At the end, they all join in.

Cock Robin

Cock Robin is dead and he lies in his bed,
oh he lies in his bed,
oh he lies in his bed.
Cock Robin is dead and he lies in his bed,
A – E – I – O̲ – U.

They have planted an apple tree over his head
... etc.

The apples got red and they all tumbled off,
... etc.

There came an old woman a picking them up,
... etc.

Cock Robin got up and he gave her a thump,
... etc.

Which made that old woman go hupperty hump,
... etc.

Bibliography

'Bangali Polton', *Indian Military History Journal*.

Chaudhuri, Gen J.N., *Memoirs*.

'Brief History of 49th', *Peace and Security Review*, Vol. 4, No .7, 2011 (BIPS S).

Hansard, 10.8.1920.

Menezes, Lt Gen S.L., *Fidelity and Honour: The Indian Army from the Seventeenth to the Twenty-first Century*, Oxford University Press, 1999.

Further Reading

Nicholson, Virginia, *Singled Out*, Viking, 2007.

Richards, Anthony, *In Their Own Words: Untold stories of the First World War*, Imperial War Museum, 2016.

Stone, Clara (alias Dr Michael West), *Death in Cranford*, Hutchinson, 1959.

Index

180

INDEX

INDEX